Critical Race Theory in Action

This book presents an expansive collection of case studies focused on Critical Race Theory (CRT), offering insights into understanding racial oppression and its societal impacts. Featuring contributions from expert practitioner–scholars, chapters introduce core tenets of CRT and explore how CRT can be applied across a range of different contexts, providing practical examples of how CRT can be implemented into the curriculum. By dividing its case studies at the micro, mezzo, and macro level, the text demonstrates how CRT is relevant for different levels of social work practice and contributes to ongoing movements to apply an anti-oppressive approach into all areas of social work. The first book of its kind, this is an essential resource for anyone seeking to develop their knowledge and explore how CRT can be used to enhance social work practice across a range of different settings.

Monique A. Constance-Huggins is a critical race scholar, who has devoted much of her academic life to exploring the theory and advancing its inclusion in social work education. She is currently a professor in the Department of Social Work at Winthrop University, where she also serves as the undergraduate Program Director.

Emily C. Pate is a Licensed Master Social Worker with experience in program implementation and evaluation in a nonprofit organization setting. She is also a Certified Financial Social Worker and works with single mothers to increase their financial literacy and employability through financial coaching, case management, and community referral coordination.

Critical Race Theory in Action

Knowledge and Application in Social Work Practice

Edited by
Monique A. Constance-Huggins
Winthrop University, South Carolina

Emily C. Pate
Winthrop University, South Carolina

Shaftesbury Road, Cambridge CB2 8EA, United Kingdom

One Liberty Plaza, 20th Floor, New York, NY 10006, USA

477 Williamstown Road, Port Melbourne, VIC 3207, Australia

314–321, 3rd Floor, Plot 3, Splendor Forum, Jasola District Centre, New Delhi – 110025, India

103 Penang Road, #05-06/07, Visioncrest Commercial, Singapore 238467

Cambridge University Press is part of Cambridge University Press & Assessment, a department of the University of Cambridge.

We share the University's mission to contribute to society through the pursuit of education, learning and research at the highest international levels of excellence.

www.cambridge.org
Information on this title: www.cambridge.org/9781009592956

DOI: 10.1017/9781009592932

© Monique A. Constance-Huggins and Emily C. Pate 2026

This publication is in copyright. Subject to statutory exception and to the provisions of relevant collective licensing agreements, no reproduction of any part may take place without the written permission of Cambridge University Press & Assessment.

When citing this work, please include a reference to the DOI 10.1017/9781009592932

First published 2026

© Original cover artwork created by Lenique Kori La-Fleur Huggins

A catalogue record for this publication is available from the British Library

A Cataloging-in-Publication data record for this book is available from the Library of Congress

ISBN 978-1-009-59295-6 Hardback
ISBN 978-1-009-59290-1 Paperback

Cambridge University Press & Assessment has no responsibility for the persistence or accuracy of URLs for external or third-party internet websites referred to in this publication and does not guarantee that any content on such websites is, or will remain, accurate or appropriate.

For EU product safety concerns, contact us at Calle de José Abascal, 56, 1°, 28003 Madrid, Spain, or email eugpsr@cambridge.org

Contents

About the Editors	*page* viii
List of Contributors	x
Acknowledgments	xvii

Part I Introduction — 1
    Critical Race Theory — 3
    Monique A. Constance-Huggins

    CRT in Social Work — 6
    Rationale for the Book — 6
    Using the Case Method in the Classroom — 8
    Organization of the Book — 9

Part II Case Studies in Micro-Level Practice — 15

Case 2.1 Oh, That's Just Endemic Racism: Application in Clinical Practice — 17
Nathaniel L. Currie

Case 2.2 Medical Mistrust in the Black Community: Navigating Endemic Racism in Medicine and Child Welfare — 28
Ebony N. Perez

Case 2.3 Adversity at the Crossroads: Navigating the Challenges of Transgender Homelessness — 40
Ashley R. Garrick

Case 2.4 Where Is My Voice? — 52
Alicia O. Tetteh

Part III Case Studies in Mezzo-Level Practice — 59

Case 3.1 White Privilege at the Work Opportunity Center — 61
Monique A. Constance-Huggins

Case 3.2 You Got What? Liberalism in a Community-Based Agency — 70
Nicole E. Vazquez

Case 3.3 Making Visible the Invisible: Intersectionality and Counter Storytelling of Black Girls in the Youth Justice System — 81
Karen M. Kolivoski and Sherri Y. Simmons-Horton

Case 3.4 What Am I Missing? The Role of Intersectionality in Child Welfare Practice and Professional Relationships — 97
Kori R. Bloomquist

Case 3.5 Don't Forget to Shine! The Intersection of Race, Age, and Sexuality at the End of Life — 111
Sara J. English

Part IV Case Studies in Macro-Level Practice — 123

Case 4.1 What's in It for Us? A Case of Interest Convergence — 125
Monique A. Constance-Huggins

Case 4.2 Hoʻokuaʻāina: Reclaiming Land, Culture, and Indigenous Voice to Advance Well-Being — 135
Susan L. Nakaoka

Case 4.3 Advancing the Voices of Those Who Are Marginalized: A Macro Intervention to Prevent Dating Violence and Intersecting Racial and Sexual Identity Disparities in New Mexico — 150
Anna N. Nelson

Case 4.4 The Great Divide: A Neighborhood's Quest of Racial Lines and Property Lines — 164
ZaDonna M. Slay

Case 4.5 You Can't Budget Your Way out of Racism: How 179
the Endemic Nature of Racism Perpetuates
Financial Instability among Black Single Mothers
Emily C. Pate

Index 188

About the Editors

Dr. Monique A. Constance-Huggins, PhD, MSW, MPIA, is a critical race scholar who has devoted much of her academic life to exploring the theory and advancing its inclusion in social work education. She received her Master of Social Work, Master in Public and International Affairs, and PhD in Social Work from the University of Pittsburgh. She is a professor in the Department of Social Work at Winthrop University, where she also serves as the Undergraduate Program Director. Dr. Constance-Huggins teaches courses in social welfare policy, working with multicultural populations, research methods, and international social work practice. As a critical race scholar, she has conducted numerous workshops and presentations, as well as written several journal articles and book chapters on CRT in social work education and practice. Her scholarship also focuses on the related areas of social, economic, and environmental justice. She also explores social capital among single women in poverty. Specifically, she is intrigued by the ways in which low-income women find agency in their social network as they respond to inadequate social policies and programs. Additionally, Dr. Constance-Huggins conducts social policy analysis for Commonwealth Caribbean countries, thereby bringing attention to the social justice implications in social processes.

Emily C. Pate, LMSW, CFSW, is a two-time graduate of Winthrop University and a Licensed Master Social Worker. She received her Bachelor of Social Work in 2022 and her Master of Social Work in 2023 and is a current member of the National Association of Social Workers. Her experience includes working with the aging population in rehabilitation and long-term care settings as well as grant-writing and program implementation and evaluation in a non-profit organization setting. Her graduate-level capstone focused on the feminization of poverty and how it specifically pertains to Black single mothers in the United States. Additionally, Pate used the research gathered for this paper to develop a proposed intervention on removing barriers to financial stability for Black single mothers, including unaffordable childcare and lack of workforce development/career advancement opportunities. Pate is also a Certified Financial Social Worker (CFSW) through the Center for Financial Social Work and works with single mothers to increase their financial literacy and employability through financial coaching, case management, and community referral coordination.

Contributors

Kori R. Bloomquist, PhD, LMSW, received her Bachelor of Social Work, Master of Social Work, and her PhD in social work from Indiana University. She has over ten years of direct practice experience in child welfare and additional practice experience in mental health, disability services, and gerontology. Dr. Bloomquist's areas of scholarship include pre-adoptive placement disruption, adoption from foster care, state child welfare evaluation, Title IV-E projects, Adverse Childhood Experiences (ACEs), attitudes on poverty and social class, and social worker self-care and professional well-being. Some of her areas of teaching expertise include generalist practice, leadership, and child welfare policy and practice.

Nathaniel L. Currie, DSW, MSW, LCSW, is a clinical social worker and educator with over fifteen years of social work experience in behavioral health, HIV, LGBTQ issues, and social justice/liberation work. He received his doctorate in social work from the University of Pennsylvania, Philadelphia, and his Master of Social Work degree from Simmons University, Boston. Dr. Currie is a licensed psychotherapist and maintains a small private practice in Atlanta. His social work practice and leadership experience includes Johns Hopkins Medicine in Baltimore, Maryland, SMYAL in Washington, D.C., and multiple FQHC and community-based agencies in Baltimore, Boston, District of Columbia, and Los Angeles. He is an assistant professor of social work and social welfare policy at Clark Atlanta University, and Adjunct Professor in the Graduate School of Social Work at Winthrop University. He tours, lectures, trains, and writes regularly on the intersection of critical race theory and social work practice, diversity, and on trauma-related topics.

Sara J. English, PhD, MSW, is an assistant professor of social work and the faculty advisor for the Gerontology Minor Program at Winthrop University. Dr. English received her Master of Social Work from Winthrop University, her BA in Behavioral Science from Columbia College, and her PhD in social work from the University of South Carolina. She is a Certified Gerontology Professional (CGP) and AGE-SW fellow. She serves as the NASW-SC representative to the Alzheimer's Advisory Board for the SC Lieutenant Governor's Office on Aging and was recognized by the NASW-SC as the Social Work Educator of the Year for 2022. Dr. English studies the power of non-familial relationships among staff and residents of institutional settings and is examining younger residents living in long-term care.

Ashley R. Garrick, MSW, LISW-CP, is a licensed clinical social worker who received her Master of Social Work from the University of Michigan in 2013, where she focused on Community Organization with Children and Youth. She earned both a Bachelor of Social Work degree and a Bachelor of Arts degree in Psychology in 2011 from Winthrop University. Garrick has specialized in empowering vulnerable and disadvantaged populations and is actively involved with local task forces and groups focused on improving outcomes for those experiencing poverty and homelessness. Garrick is currently the Associate Field Director and Instructor at Winthrop University where she believes in active engagement and incorporating students' unique voices and perspectives into their learning experience.

Karen M. Kolivoski, **PhD, MSW**, received her Master of Social Work and PhD in social work from the University of Pittsburgh and was a postdoctoral fellow in the School of Social Work at the University of Maryland, Baltimore, the Deputy Director for Research at the Center for Juvenile Justice Reform (CJJR) at the McCourt School of Public Policy at Georgetown University and a Distinguished Fellow of Juvenile Justice at Child Trends in the Youth Development department. Previously, she was an associate professor in the Communities, Administration, and Policy Practice concentration at the School of Social Work at Howard University and the Lead Data Consultant for the Crossover Youth Practice Model (CYPM) at CJJR. Her research aims to advance social justice through structural changes that affect the lives of children, youth, and families who experience involvement in multiple systems, specifically the child welfare, juvenile, and criminal legal systems. Dr. Kolivoski has also been named a research fellow for the Society for Social Work and Research (SSWR). She is chair of the Criminal and Juvenile Justice track for the Council on Social Work Education (CSWE) Annual Program Meeting (APM).

Susan L. Nakaoka, PhD, MSW, **MA**, is the Director of Practicum Education in the Department of Social Welfare at University of California, Los Angeles (UCLA). As a third-generation Japanese American/Chicana, her family's World War II incarceration informs her teaching, scholarship, and commitment to racial justice. Dr. Lares-Nakaoka's research and writing focuses on the intersection of race and community development, critical race pedagogy, and Asian American and Pacific Islander communities. She is also an editor of the 2024 special issue of the Journal of Community Practice on race and social justice entitled, "Necessary Interventions: 'Racing' Community Practice." Dr. Lares-Nakaoka is co-founder and co-director of the Critical Race Scholars in Social Work (CRSSW) collective. Her experience as Director of Practicum Education at California State University (CSU) Dominguez Hills, the first MSW program with a critical race theory perspective, was foundational to her approach to social work pedagogy. Prior to coming to UCLA, she was an assistant professor at the University of Hawaii, CSU Sacramento, and CSU Long Beach.

Anna N. Nelson, PhD, LCSW, is a critical race scholar, a contributing researcher for critical trauma theory, an educator and social work practitioner, and director for the New Mexico Highlands University Facundo Valdez School of Social Work Center for Excellence in Social Work. Her clinical expertise is in adolescent behavioral health. Her research interests are the cooccurrence of exposure to racism, risk for ethnoracial, oppression-based, cumulative, cultural, and collective traumas and the simultaneous expression of cultural and identity capital and community cultural wealth for Black, Indigenous and People and Communities of Color and LGBTQQIA2S+ Peoples. Dr. Nelson is an advisory board member for the national Critical Race Scholars in Social Work Network. For her work in promoting racial justice and equity in education, Dr. Nelson is the recipient of the New Mexico Education Equity Alliance (NMEEA) 2013 Annual Fueling Increasingly Relevant Education (F.I.R.E) Award, the YWCA-NM Women on the Move to Eliminate Racism Award in 2015, the New Mexico State University "A" Mountain Award in 2020, and the New Mexico State University Teaching Excellence Award in 2023.

Ebony N. Perez, PhD, MSW, currently serves as a Tenured Assistant Professor of Undergraduate Social Work and Department Chair at Saint Leo University. Her research agenda focuses on the nuances and complexities of the role of social work educators in advancing inclusive and transformative policies and preparing future practitioners for anti-racist praxis. Dr. Perez has over fifteen years of experience in social work practice and has held various roles including Behavioral Specialist, Research Associate, Inpatient Psychiatric Social Worker, and Pediatric ICU Social Worker. She received her PhD in Curriculum and Instruction: Higher Education Administration and a graduate certificate in Diversity in Education from the University of South Florida (USF) and her Master of Social Work degree at the University of Pittsburgh School of Social Work. In addition to scholarship and research, Dr. Perez has served on community boards and is currently serving as a member of the Council on Social Work Education (CSWE) Council on Racial, Ethnic, and Cultural Diversity. Her work has been presented at multiple national and international conferences, including at the American Educational Research Association, the Association for the Study of Higher Education, CSWE, and The Learner Conference. Her research has been published in *Advances in Social Work, Journal of Ethnic and*

Cultural Diversity in Social Work, Journal of College Development, and has several book chapters.

Sherri Y. Simmons-Horton, PhD, MSW, is an assistant professor in the Social Work Department at the University of New Hampshire (UNH). She also serves as a Core Faculty member in the Women and Gender Studies Department at UNH. Simmons-Horton has over twenty-five years of practice experience in the child welfare system in the state of Texas, with a focus on addressing racism and racial disparities present for Black children, youth, and families. Simmons-Horton's research explores experiences of Black crossover youth in family policing and juvenile legal systems, primarily through the lens of Black feminism and other anti-racist frameworks. Her scholarship further examines and interrogates structural inequities across both systems and highlights empowerment among Black adolescents. Simmons-Horton serves as the 2nd Vice President of the Black Administrators in Child Welfare, and she is a staunch child, family, and youth activist, with a strong interest in practice and policy strategies to dismantle oppressive practices in the child welfare and juvenile justice systems.

ZaDonna M. Slay, DSW, MSW, earned her Bachelor of Science in Social Work from Savannah State University, her Master of Social Work from the University of South Carolina, and her Doctor of Social Work from the University of St. Thomas. Her highlighted publications include "Sex Trafficking of Black Girls: A Critical Race Theory Approach to Practice." Her areas of expertise include voting rights and empowerment, non-profit management, Black women disparity, strong Black women schema, and Black feminist perspective. Dr. Slay has over a decade of professional experience in youth development, social welfare policy issues, and non-profit management. In 2019, she was selected as a United State of Women Ambassador. In this volunteer role, she worked with community agencies and organizations toward voter equity and engagement for women and provided education and awareness on overall disparity issues for Black women.

List of Contributors

Alicia O. Tetteh, DSW, LCSW, identifies as a change agent. She sits at the intersection of clinical practice and academia. Dr. Tetteh completed her Bachelor of Social Work degree at Virginia Commonwealth University, her Master of Social Work Degree at Howard University, and her Doctorate of Social Work from Simmons University. Dr. Tetteh is an assistant professor at Norfolk State University and has a private practice, "Building Endurance," where she sees outpatient clients and does some consulting. Dr. Tetteh's research focus is helping leaders and organizations practice from an anti-racist lens as well as financial well-being and trauma. Her clinical focus is helping individuals navigate through current and intergenerational trauma. Dr. Tetteh is certified in Trauma-Focused Cognitive Behavioral Therapy, Brainspotting, and EMDR. She is a board-approved clinical supervisor for social workers and counselors as well as an approved EMDR consultant. She has a published chapter in *Black Faculty Do It All: A Moment in the Life of a Blackademic*. Connecting with the community around mindfulness, navigating through trauma, and awareness of the impact of caring for our mental health are some of her platforms. Dr. Tetteh is a member of the National Association of Social Work, the Association of Black Social Workers, and Delta Sigma Theta Sorority Incorporated.

Nicole E. Vazquez, MSW, MPP, is a queer Afro-Latinx cisgender woman of Mexican-American and Panamanian parents. She holds dual Masters degrees in Social Welfare and Public Policy from University of California, Los Angeles, where she was first introduced to Critical Race Theory (CRT). She specializes in the practical application of CRT, with an emphasis on social work practice. She is co-founder and co-director of the Critical Race Scholars in Social Work Collective, and she has over twenty-five years' experience that includes work with elected officials, in government agencies and in grassroots organizations. Her direct practice experience includes crisis counseling, in-home counseling, and case management. As the CEO of Amor Adelante, Vazquez centers and advances love in all her work that includes merchandising, exploration, and discovery with individuals and organizations on the road to transformation through dialogues, workshops, program assessment, strategic planning, and conflict mediation. She approaches all her work with love, humility, and as a learner.

Acknowledgments

We would like to thank the many authors who contributed their work to this book, and who continue to advance critical race theory (CRT) in social work. Without your commitment to advancing the important work of CRT, this project would not have been possible. We would also like to thank the many students and practitioners who, over the years, have continued to ask for content on how CRT can be used as a lens to assess and address issues in all levels of social work practice. Your thirst for this content has truly served as the impetus for this book. Lastly, we would like to thank our families for creating the space for us to work on this project.

PART I
Introduction

Critical Race Theory

MONIQUE A. CONSTANCE-HUGGINS

Critical Race Theory (CRT) brings attention to the centrality of race and racism as impactful social processes in society. The theory first emerged in the field of law in the 1970s when two scholars, Richard Delgado and Derrick Bell, began to ponder over the reasons for the lack of progress on race equality following the civil rights movement. They purport that the movement had not brought about the extent of changes in racial outcomes as was anticipated because of how racism is intricately embedded in all aspects of society. Seven common tenets guide CRT. These are: racism is endemic; social construction of race; critique of liberalism; interest convergence; white privilege; intersectionality; and advancing the voice of those who are marginalized.

The tenet of *racism is endemic* purports that race is deeply entrenched in all aspects of society. This implies that race plays out in our beliefs, attitudes, behavior, and policies, which manifest themselves in every sphere of life including health, wealth, income, education, homeownership, and many others. *Social construction* is another tenet of CRT. It refers to the ways that we assign meaning to people and problems. For example, society may assign terms such as good, clean, intelligent, and innocent to White people, while assigning bad, dirty, poor, and guilty to Black individuals (Butler, 2015). The meanings assigned to groups of people are then used to determine how they are treated and the kinds of policies that are put in place to target them. For example, if Black girls are labeled as "fast" and promiscuous, then cases of sex trafficking involving them would not be taken seriously, as there would be a tendency to blame the victim (Constance-Huggins et al., 2021).

Also, CRT *critiques liberalism and the neutrality of law*. Specifically, it critiques the idea of color blindness, which was one of the most common racial ideologies in the 1960s. The notion of color blindness suggests that since race should not matter in society, it does not matter. It essentially implies that we do not see color, and that discrimination does not exist. This ideology is challenged by CRT, suggesting that although race should not matter in determining someone's outcome, it does in fact still matter in society. This is evident in the persistent and deep color-coded disparities that exist in every aspect of society. For example, racial disparity is evident in education, homeownership, health, wealth, and many other areas. Neville et al. (2000) suggest that to be color-blind is to deny that discrimination exists and to overlook the lived experiences of racial minorities.

The CRT tenet of *interest convergence* draws attention to the support of policies that benefit minoritized groups. It suggests that dominant culture will only support policies and programs aimed at benefiting minority groups if they also stand to benefit. An often-cited example of interest convergence is the case regarding *Brown vs Board of Education*. While the support for desegregation was to advance Black individuals, the decision at the same time benefited the US as a whole, as it allowed them to improve their image on the world stage during the Cold War era. Essentially, CRT surmises that although minoritized groups stand to benefit from certain decisions, the principal focus is on advancing the desires and positions of the dominant group (Delgado & Stefancic, 2012). Accordingly, the concerns and interests of minoritized groups are decentered.

Another tenet of CRT is *White privilege*. This suggests that White individuals have unearned advantages due to their skin color. For example, they enjoy the privilege of being assumed to be more creditworthy, to be more honest, or to be more innocent relative to their Black counterparts. They have the privilege of not being followed closely while shopping because of the assumption of being a shoplifter. In her article, "White Privilege: Unpacking the Invisible Knapsack," Peggy McIntosh (2003) drew attention to the multiple ways in which having white skin confers benefits on individuals, and conversely, how people of color experience burdens because of their skin color. According to CRT, these burdens significantly hamper the social and economic advancement of racial minorities.

The tenet of *intersectionality* acknowledges that we are more than one identity. For example, an individual is not just Black, but can be a woman, disabled, and poor at the same time. Accordingly, the tenet speaks to the ways that different aspects of one's identity interact to complicate their lived experiences. This concept was popularized by Kimberlé Crenshaw (1988), who recognized that Black women, who sat at the intersection of their gender and race, were excluded from conversations pertaining to women and to Black people. Specifically, literature on women and feminism tended to highlight the experiences of White women, while literature on Black people focused more on the experiences of Black men. Accordingly, the intersectionality approach allows society to see the unique experiences of Black women and others with their intersecting identities. Patricia Hill Collins (1990) added to the discourse on intersectionality by drawing attention to the intersection of oppressed identities. She noted that the matrix of domination occurs when multiple oppressed identities intersect, leading to poorer outcomes for such individuals. For example, a person who is in a racial minority, is gay, has a disability, and is poor will experience more discrimination and worse outcomes than their counterparts, with fewer disadvantaged identities.

The tenet of *advancing the voice* of those who are marginalized acknowledges the fact that racial minorities are often not heard and afforded the opportunity to tell their truth. The tenet acknowledges that minoritized groups are best positioned to tell their story. It posits that the absence of Black voices can result in stories about the population that are diluted and incorrect.

CRT in Social Work

Although CRT did not have its roots in social work, over the years, the profession has made significant progress in incorporating it into its practice, teaching, and research. Early scholars such as Ortiz and Jani (2010) and Constance-Huggins (2013) spoke about the need to include CRT into social work education. They critiqued the multicultural approach, stating that while it draws attention to the differences between groups, it does not shed light on the oppression that groups face and the resulting disparities between groups. Accordingly, they posit that multicultural education did not spur people to take social action. In addition to making a case for CRT in social work education, scholars like Kolivoski et al. (2014), made a case for its application to social work practice. They provided examples of how it can be applied to mental health services, child welfare, and public assistance work.

Rationale for the Book

Racial disparities and racial injustice remain daunting social problems in today's society. The impacts of these are deep and multifaceted. Given the persistence and the deep impact of these issues, social workers, who are change agents, must continue to equip themselves with the knowledge and skills needed to address oppressive behaviors. In fact, the 2022 Council on Social Work Education (CSWE) Educational Policy and Accreditation

Standards (EPAS) (CSWE, 2022), has drawn greater attention to the need for social work students to develop anti-racist and anti-oppressive competencies. One anti-racist framework that centers race and racism and is consistent with the values and aims of social work is CRT, which draws attention to the mechanism of race and racism in shaping the lived experiences of people of color (Delgado, 1995). Social work scholars such as Constance-Huggins (2013), and Ortiz and Jani (2010) have called for a greater infusion of CRT into social work education. Although it is slowly being infused into the curriculum, there is a lack of textbooks that provide students with practical examples of how CRT can be implemented. Further, there are currently no case study books that use CRT as a framework for case assessment. Students often lament that while they embrace CRT, they do not feel equipped to apply it. This signals the need for more focus on the implementation of this very important framework in social work practice. This current text is intended to fill the gap.

Facing the Grand Challenges of CRT

In recent years, CRT has faced significant challenges, which have served to undermine its importance and impact. This section offers what appears to be four grand challenges of CRT, which fuel the need for the current book. The first challenge is the anti-CRT climate in which we find ourselves. CRT has been labeled by some policymakers as a divisive phenomenon that threatens to infect core institutions and cause chaos in our country. This narrative has been etched in the minds of many Americans who now view CRT as offensive and something to resist.

The second challenge is the fear of faculty, and in particular, junior faculty, to embrace CRT in their teaching and research. Faculty might want to stay "safe" and not publish content on the topic for fear that it could affect their university tenure. The unfortunate reality is that if faculty members do not publish and teach about CRT, students may not learn the truth about it.

A third challenge of CRT is the "brownie point mentality." Institutions may be simply looking for diversity brownie points rather than having real inclusion. If they are merely interested in brownie points, they may be less supportive of efforts to advance CRT as well as fail to acknowledge the lived experiences of racial minorities. It then becomes a situation of gaining diversity but shunning inclusion. A fourth challenge is the disproportionate service burden that faculty of color, and more so, Black women, carry in academia. According to Asare (2024), Black faculty are more likely to serve on diversity committees, mentor students from marginalized backgrounds, and do other things to help create an inclusive space. This is despite the fact that everyone, not just racial minorities, has a role to play in the advancement of social justice. This results in significant burnout among faculty of color, and eventually erosion of the fight for social justice.

Using the Case Method in the Classroom

This case study book offers important insight into CRT, how race shows up in different contexts, and how CRT can appropriately be applied in these contexts. We asked contributors to write cases that highlight the use of particular tenets of CRT in analyzing and responding to race-related social problems. These cases, written by social workers and teachers, reflect the utility of CRT at the micro, mezzo, and macro levels of social work practice. The cases are either based on real scenarios or are realistic adaptations to advance understanding of CRT in viewing and addressing a problem.

The book acts as a supplemental guide rather than a stand-alone textbook. This book contains cases and discussion points that can be applied to many different courses throughout a social work program. This means that the book may be used throughout an entire curriculum rather than be relegated to a single class on diversity.

Accordingly, it can make a more meaningful contribution to student learning.

Educators can use each chapter of the book to introduce the students to a particular tenet of CRT. The case study book can also be used following a lecture on a particular area of social work such as mental health, homelessness, public assistance, child welfare, disaster recovery, among others, to demonstrate how race complicates the lived experiences of people of color. The implications for social work practice content and the discussion questions provided at the end of each case can provide students with a framework for analyzing the case, and for thinking critically about how CRT can be applied in their future work. Educators are encouraged to use additional questions as they see fit.

Organization of the Book

The case study book has four parts. The first part is an introduction to CRT and the book. Parts II, III, and IV are divided into micro, mezzo, and macro, respectively, to reflect the major areas of social work practice. Each of these parts has four or five cases, with each of the cases presenting a study that highlights a tenet of CRT. The cases begin with a brief description of the highlighted CRT tenet, followed by the case example, a brief discussion of the implication of that tenet for social work practice, and end with some discussion questions. Although every practice level does not contain every tenet, each part/section discusses real-world examples of the importance of practicing through a CRT lens, and each CRT tenet is covered throughout the book. Some tenets are intentionally repeated across different parts/sections of the book, thereby indicating how these can be manifested at different levels of social work practice. The CRT tenets that are covered throughout the case study book are: racism is endemic, white privilege, the critique of liberalism, interest convergence, race as a social construct, intersectionality, and advancing the voice of marginalized individuals.

Part II presents micro-level cases. Micro-level practice typically involves individualized, one-on-one work with a client or family. Part II contains four cases covering the following tenets: racism is endemic, intersectionality, advancing the voice of the marginalized, and white privilege. The first case (2.1), "Oh That's Just Endemic Racism: Application in Clinical Practice," focuses on a case highlighting the tenet of racism being endemic on a micro level, following a Black, gay man facing prejudice within the military as well as his family. The case shows how an individual's life is compounded because of the way racism is embedded into the fabric of society and manifests itself through everyday social processes. The second case (2.2), "Medical Mistrust in the Black Community: Navigating Endemic Racism in Medicine and Child Welfare," discusses how racism being endemic affects Black individuals' likelihood to trust the medical system. The third case (2.3), "Adversity at the Crossroads: Navigating the Challenges of Transgender Homelessness," focuses on the CRT tenet of intersectionality at the micro level regarding the issue of homelessness. Informed by the work of Kimberlé Crenshaw (1988) on intersectionality and Patricia Hill Collins (1990), this case highlights how the intersectionality of multiple oppressed identities compounds the life of an individual. Case 2.4, "Where Is My Voice?" highlights advancing the voice of the marginalized in a clinical/mental health setting, following a Black woman facing adversity in the workplace and how she develops skills in therapy to address her mental health.

Part III focuses on mezzo cases. Mezzo-level practice involves providing services and implementing social programs in small groups, organizations, or neighborhoods. Part III includes five cases covering the following tenets: white privilege, social construction, intersectionality, and critique of liberalism. The first case (3.1) is titled "White Privilege at the Work Opportunity Center" and discusses how White privilege penetrates the welfare system in an unsuspecting way. "You Got What? Liberalism in a

Community-Based Agency," Case 3.2, critiques liberalism in a case about best serving a Latinx community. Case 3.3 is titled "Making Visible the Invisible: Intersectionality and Counter Storytelling of Black Girls in the Youth Justice System." Through the lens of CRT tenet intersectionality, this case describes how a social worker empowers Black girls in the Youth Justice System through counter storytelling. Case 3.4 is titled, "What Am I Missing? The Role of Intersectionality in Child Welfare Practice and Professional Relationships." This case highlights intersectionality on a mezzo level, and how it pertains to child welfare – specifically in terms of reunification. Case 3.5, "Don't Forget to Shine! The Intersection of Race, Age, and Sexuality at the End of Life" discusses race as a social construction through a case about an elderly trans Black woman in a nursing home setting.

Lastly, Part IV draws attention to macro cases. Macro-level practice helps vulnerable populations indirectly and on larger-scale issues, such as city, state, national, or international-wide social inequities. Part IV includes five cases covering the following tenets: interest convergence, racism is endemic, critique of liberalism, and advancing the voice of the marginalized. Case 4.1, "What's In It for Us? A Case of Interest Convergence," highlights interest convergence in St. Vincent and the Grenadines and provides an example of how practices that benefit minoritized groups are supported by dominant cultures as they also stand to benefit from these practices in major ways. Next, Case 4.2, "Ho'okua'āina: Reclaiming Land, Culture and Indigenous Voice to Advance Well-Being," highlights the tenet of advancing the voice of the marginalized. It follows a case of Native Hawaiian community building, providing an innovative and powerful approach to strengths-based practice that has societal-level impact. Case 4.3 is titled "Advancing the Voices of Those Who Are Marginalized: A Macro Intervention to Prevent Dating Violence and Intersecting Racial and Sexual Identity Disparities in New Mexico." This case gives insight on how to uplift the voices of Black, Indigenous, Latinx, and youth of color to prevent dating violence.

Case 4.4, "The Great Divide: A Neighborhood's Quest of Racial Lines and Property Lines," uses CRT's critique of liberalism to discuss a struggling HOA community in need of intervention. The final case (4.5), "You Can't Budget Your Way out of Racism: How the Endemic Nature of Racism Perpetuates Financial Instability among Black Single Mothers," discusses the ways in which Black single mothers disproportionately face financial instability and how a systems-level intervention is needed to address this issue.

REFERENCES

Asare, J. (2024). Academia Is Failing Black Women: Examining Misogynoir within the Academy. Forbes Newsletter. www.forbes.com/sites/janicegassam/2024/01/16/academia-is-failing-black-women-a-brief-examination-of-misogynoir-within-the-academy/

Butler, C. N. (2015). The racial roots of human trafficking. UCLA Law Review. Online. www.uclalawreview.org/racial-roots-human-trafficking/

Constance-Huggins, M. (2013). Critical race theory in social work education: A framework for addressing racial disparities. *Critical Social Work*, *13*(2), 1–16. https://doi.org/10.22329/csw.v13i2.5861

Constance-Huggins, M., Moore, S., & Slay, Z. (2021). Sex trafficking of Black girls: A critical race theory approach to practice. *Journal of Progressive Human Services* *33*(1), 62–74. https://doi.org/10.1080/10428232.2021.1987755

Council on Social Work Education. (2022). Educational Policy and Accreditation Standards for Baccalaureate and Master's Social Work Programs. Council on Social Work Education. www.cswe.org/getmedia/bb5d8afe-7680-42dc-a332-a6e6103f4998/2022-EPAS.pdf

Crenshaw, K. W. (1988). Race, reform, and retrenchment: Transformation and legitimation in antidiscrimination law. *Harvard Law Review*, *101*, 1331–1387.

Delgado, R. (1995). *Critical race theory: The cutting edge.* Temple University Press.

Delgado, R., & Stefancic, J. (2012). *Critical race theory: An introduction* (2nd ed.). New York University Press.

Hill Collins, P. (1990). *Black feminist thought: Knowledge, consciousness, and the politics of empowerment.* Unwin Hyman.

Kolivoski, K. M., Weaver, A., & Constance-Huggins, M. (2014). Critical Race Theory: Opportunities for application in social work practice and policy.

Families in Society, 95(4), 269-276. https://doi.org/10.1606/1044-3894.2014.95.36

McIntosh, P. (2003). White privilege: Unpacking the invisible knapsack. In S. Plous (Ed.), *Understanding prejudice and discrimination* (pp. 191-196). McGraw-Hill.

Neville, H., Lilly, R., Lee, R., Duran, G., & Browne, L. (2000). Construction and initial validation of the color-blind racial attitude scale. *Journal of Counseling Psychology, 47*(1), 59-70. https://doi.org/10.1037/0022-0167.47.1.59

Ortiz, L., & Jani, J. (2010). Critical race theory: A transformational model for teaching diversity. *Journal of Social Work Education, 46*(2), 175-193.

PART II

Case Studies in
Micro-Level Practice

CASE 2.1

Oh, That's Just Endemic Racism
Application in Clinical Practice

NATHANIEL L. CURRIE

Introduction

If we conceptualize individual racism as biases, prejudices, stereotypes, beliefs, or actions that participate in, collude, or perpetuate racist ideology, we can have a good beginning of understanding how individual racism may show up in clinical work. It is helpful to analyze this idea in three parts: 1) how racism shows up in the client's identity, environments, and experiences; 2) how individual racism shows up in the clinician's identity, environments, experiences, and clinical practice; and lastly, 3) how individual racism shows up in the therapeutic relationship between client and therapist, and potentially informs or complicates the power differential. Primary tools in this discovery will be the clinician's own critical self-reflection, acknowledgment of their own social location, awareness of how they show up completely in the therapeutic space, and a firm understanding of both overt and covert racism.

Take the highly complex case of Donte which follows. Clinicians not trained in anti-racist and anti-oppressive practice lenses such as CRT, empowerment practice, the Afrocentric perspective, decolonization, DisCrit, QueerCrit, feminism, and other anti-oppressive lenses might solely assess and remark on the environmental and clinical aspects of the case, leaving the influences of race and racism unattended. Donte's experiences of oppression in his childhood, young adulthood, as well as covertly by systems he has interacted with, have a direct impact on his mental health and on his success in treatment Practicing scholars have identified racism itself as traumatic, in what is termed *socially engineered trauma,* due to its psychological, physiological, environmental, and social effects on an individual self (Currie, 2026; Shaia et al., 2019). Socially engineered traumas are defined as traumatic events rooted in social forces of oppression and inequality. Social work's focus on trauma's micro-level experience over its macro-level origins limits workers' options for responding to trauma at all levels (Shaia et al., 2019). Scholars such as Wendy Shaia, and clinicians such as David Avruch, have written extensively on the importance of the concept in social work practice. If exposure to racism is experienced as trauma, then it would be clinically significant to assess how racism shows up in not just the client's life but also in their access to therapeutic care, within the clinical assessment, psychopathology/diagnosis, and treatment intervention used in their therapeutic care, and in how clinicians prepare clients to return to their environments during and post treatment. It is not enough to provide anti-oppressive therapeutic intervention for clients and then return them to the racist and oppressive environments responsible for their trauma and discord. Clinicians should strive to accommodate this need throughout the treatment process. The CRT tenet, racism as endemic, assists the clinician in exploring and remediating (or at least considering) the social and psychological effects of racism on the individual. Think of this notion as you explore the case of Donte which follows.

The Case of Donte

Donte is a twenty-five-year-old Black gay cisgender male. He is single with no children and resides in a large metropolitan area in the American South. He is gainfully employed in a medical practice. He was referred to clinic by a senior nurse colleague who encouraged him to make an appointment with a therapist to discuss his fluctuating moods, ongoing depression, and to explore his concerns with his prescribed medical and psychiatric medications. Donte agreed to make the appointment and attend. After some struggle in coordinating appointment times, he showed up for his intake session. At his first session he appeared nervous, weary, and visibly *down*. Donte did feel comfortable enough to build rapport and engaged with the therapist who was friendly and shared many of the same identity factors; some of which were easily observed by Donte.

Over his first three sessions, Donte describes his early life as generally happy. He was raised in a medium-sized town in the deep south with his parents and two sisters. Donte's family demanded strictness and explicit dedication to church and their church community. Donte had school and church friends, engaged in activities, had close relationships with cousins, and did well in grade school where he describes himself as "mostly quiet" but sometimes "had a lot of energy." He states he "always loved to run and swim, and always had lots of ideas". Some nights, as a child, when he couldn't sleep, he "would draw and sketch for hours." Donte recalls often feeling reserved around his family and church community into his late teens, knowing that he is gay and that he had romantic and sexual attraction to other young men, and presumed that his family and church community would be unaccepting of his true self. Donte constantly feared losing his family and community. Despite attending a racially diverse school, Donte recalls being "picked-on" at times by other children based on his race, recalling peers calling him names like "blacky" or "tar baby." Donte described this period of his life as when he first noticed daily feelings of anxiety and depression, which he described as "getting worse" over time.

At the age of eighteen, he opted to join the military directly out of high school for the college financial benefits and job skills, and as a way to create distance between himself and his family and home community. Having grown up in a strict Black southern Baptist household, the discipline of the military was, at first, comfortable for Donte. Further, because of his sexual/romantic orientation, he felt the continued need to validate his masculinity in a cultural and social context to his family, including in how he presented masculinity, gender role behaviors, and positioning himself as a future "provider", a identity role important and expected in Black families. The military provided this for Donte. Donte's father exclaimed to Donte before leaving for his basic training, "maybe these guys can toughen you up." Donte stated in session he hoped at first that they would.

During his time in the military, he did generally well. He never questioned authority and completed every task assigned to him quickly and meticulously. He recalls some hyperactivity and racing thoughts at this time, which he "put into his work." Despite his hard work and loyalty, he was passed over for promotions and opportunities. Eventually, he became frustrated with observing promotions of his peers, while his own was not considered. He began to speak up about this to peers and supervisors. He was denied multiple times, and each request for promotion consideration was met with additional responsibilities and discipline, along with verbal abuse. Donte recalls being taunted and called "boy" and "nigger boy" on more than one occasion or being described as "lazy" or "weak", even when he outperformed his peers in routine tasks. The pressure began to weigh on Donte, however, he continued to remain motivated; he states he was afraid to "go home as a failure." Donte observed his anxiety increase, especially as the poor treatment on base continued. Donte recalls first noticing a change in his mood at this time, feeling drastically "up and down" and feeling "very stressed and alone." After making a more direct, formal request for promotion through the proper channels and ranks, Donte was alerted he would be up for promotion. Days before the scheduled promotion occurred, Donte states he was led, at night, blindfolded, from his bunk to a cross-base location. Upon arrival, he and two other junior service members were hazed to "earn" their promotions by several senior male service members. Donte stated he and the other two junior service members had also recently been more vocal about fairness of promotions on base and had been labeled "problems." The haze included several acts or demands meant to embarrass them, and included verbal abuse, the exposure of their nude bodies, and several demeaning tasks and physical abuses. Donte described his mental health deteriorating after the hazing incidents.

Donte returned to his parents' home chronically depressed and with significant Post-Traumatic Stress Disorder (PTSD). He felt guilt, shame, and an overwhelming sense of failure. He refused to engage in mental health or HIV treatment services, which he had acquired and been diagnosed while in the army. His depression became debilitating. He slept most days and fell into a state of shock for weeks on end. He described moments of catatonia and disassociation. His depression severely increased when he was informed that a service member colleague, that had been involved in the hazing, had committed suicide.

Donte notes that during this time his mother generally cared for him, however, their relationship remained strained. Donte agreed to see a psychiatrist after weeks of pressure from his mother, in which she accompanied him. For a short time, he worked with this psychiatrist and received his first formal Bipolar I Disorder diagnosis. At the time, Donte refused to believe the diagnosis and often faked taking his prescribed medication when administered to him by his mother. Donte recalls an overall sense of failure on his return home that continued despite the events and victimization that led to his discharge. Donte also recalled at the time his family using stigma-based or disparaging words to describe his HIV diagnosis or his sexual orientation. A year after his discharge, Donte left his family home and moved to a new city where he found affordable temporary housing and a job. Donte's familial relationship remained strained.

Upon moving out of his parents' house, Donte began to drink alcohol. He found that while drinking he felt better, physically calmer, and had "less thoughts," especially in the evening. Donte struggled with emotional regulation, and because of his insight, intelligence, and dissociation, was able to speak about this in a matter-of-fact manner in session by describing in detail his feelings, reasons for using alcohol, and his unwillingness to engage with his matronal family. He recalls several previous times when he felt "down" and that he "just needed something." To meet this need, he would drink, smoke cannabis, or engage in sex/sex behaviors with multiple or back-to-back sex partners, sometimes three or four in a day.

Donte is able to demonstrate and articulate some protective factors. Donte states that a male cousin that he is close to has provided social and treatment support over the last two years, including working with him to set up protections during periods for which he experiences hypomanic episodes. One example of these supportive protective factors was working with Donte's bank to lock his savings accounts when multiple unusual transactions are made on his checking accounts, saving him the financial and emotional consequences. Another example is that Donte keeps his firearms locked in boxes at his cousin's home, where his cousin also holds one of the two keys, and can limit access when Donte is feeling unwell.

When Donte first came into our specialty medical and behavioral health program, he was not actively engaged in therapy or medication management/pharmacology. The priority problem/goal was identity as assessing readiness and working with Donte to begin both anti-retroviral therapy (ART) for the treatment of HIV and psychotropic medications for the treatment of his Bipolar I Disorder. In his first session, he stated that he worked in a care-related job in medicine and that he had income from both his job and veteran's disability. Both his job and his living arrangement, a rented room in a house with two other roommates, were both highly stressful environments triggering his mood fluctuation, which, as he describes, often changes throughout the day.

In medical records and discharge paperwork provided by Donte, he held a primary diagnosis of Bipolar I Disorder, and a secondary diagnosis of PTSD. Documentation confirmed and corroborated a history of mood instability, episodes of over activity, a history of suicidal ideation, multiple psychosocial stressors and environments, and comorbid diagnoses including substance misuse (alcohol), attention deficit hyperactivity disorder, and a historical diagnosis of an anxiety disorder. Donte and his mother also provided medication histories from multiple providers.

After about six weeks of working with Donte, he was engaged in his antiretroviral therapy treatment, weekly Cognitive Behavioral Therapy-based sessions, a yoga class regimen, and had agreed to make and keep an appointment with a local psychiatrist. After his psychiatry appointment, Donte followed up with his therapist for a fifteen-minute telephonic session to debrief the session, forward documentation, and to encourage engagement in the newly prescribed psychotropic medication regimen. During this telephonic session, Donte and his therapist also worked to reinforce his behavioral goals which include maintaining a set schedule for work, sleep, leisure, and activities of daily living (ADLs); talk therapy; positive self-talk; and journal writing. Donte also began to explore life/environmental changes, like seeking out less stressful employment and home/living environments.

Donte has shown resilience and motivation in his willingness to participate in talk therapy, which is largely responsible for Donte's readiness for and later engagement with psychiatry and psychopharmacology, antiretroviral treatment adherence, and creating and maintaining behavior modification, including establishing routines, schedules, and self-care practices. Donte has begun to use his therapy to unpack the trauma and oppression he experienced throughout his life: race-based trauma in public school, the military, and in social and resource systems. He has also begun to explore sexual/romantic orientation-based oppression experienced in his church community, family, and social systems, and HIV and mental health stigma experienced in his church community, family, and social systems, particularly in dating and pursuing a romantic relationship. Through his therapy, Donte has begun to discover how racist systems and the unintentional centering of racist and oppressive ideology in his community and family have impacted how he thinks about himself and his value, his deservingness of community, family, support, and safety, and how he both navigates and/or resists health resources.

Understanding the Problem and Intervention

In our case, you cannot talk about Donte's lived psychological, emotional, and traumatic experiences without first acknowledging how race/racial ideology and identity show up. Many practitioners will understand race as not much more than a demographic box checked off on an intake form, or regard race as simply the appearance of the client themselves. Race is more dynamic and nuanced than that. Donte's identity as a Black cisgender male requires more consideration in clinical work than simply a demographic. For example, racial profiling, workplace discrimination, health disparities, and daily exposure to microaggressions often cause Black men to distrust and experience greater inhibition when engaged in therapeutic services (Aymer, 2010; Miller & Garran, 2017). This can leave therapeutic services more fractured, strained, and likely to discontinue, leaving mental and emotional health and substance use disorder untreated. Donte himself experienced workplace discrimination, daily exposure to microaggressions, and health disparities. It should not be lost on the clinician that in 2019, 26 percent of new HIV acquisitions were among cisgender Black gay and bisexual men (CDC, 2021). Racism is a stressor to those that experience it. Long-term exposure to stress and distress can produce long-term chronic stress disorders and or exacerbate trauma or post-traumatic stress disorders (PTSD). Countless studies have shown the direct links of racism and oppression, even intergenerational experience of racism and oppression, to chronic stress disorders. It is clear that Donte's exposure to race-based oppression and other exposures to stress have compounded to exacerbate his chronic stress disorder. Chronic stress disorders like PTSD have a myriad of negative health consequences including physiological, physical, cognitive, emotional, interpersonal, and behavioral. Simply put, prolonged exposure to racism has serious health consequences. Further, in treating Black men like Donte, intentional engagement, particularly by other clinicians of color, development of trust, validation of experiences of racism and oppression throughout treatment, sustained work, aligning cultural and spiritual values, and creating safety within the therapeutic alliance may offer a more comprehensive and successful experience.

Implications for Clinical Practice

Race is a social construction necessary for racism, which has a concrete existence, impact, and profound social and psychological consequences (Miller & Garran, 2017). Thus, CRT provides a framework for examining power structures that maintain racial inequities and developing strategies for action and change (Kolivoski et al., 2014). Further, socially constructed racial categories that perpetuate stereotypes while ignoring scientific fact are invented, manipulated, and retired when convenient for those in power. To challenge institutional or cultural racism, CRT promotes a realist view of American social structures, emphasizing open acknowledgment of the dominant role that race has historically played and continues to play in society (Bell, 1995; Kolivoski et al., 2014). Clients of color will often relate to and appreciate, while also being challenged by, this "realist view" approach. For clinicians, the CRT tenet of racism as ordinary/endemic is likely to provide a framework for examining race, racism, and power within clinical and clinical case management work and their subsequent implications for clients and their families. At a baseline, American therapeutic practice is centered in and reflects dominant Eurocentric cultural values. Schools of social work and psychology largely teach counseling theory and practice developed out of the experiences of White clinicians and researchers working with almost exclusively White participants (Miller & Garran, 2017). The tenet of *racism is ordinary/endemic* demands that clinicians recognize and analyze the limits of Eurocentric theory, models, and research, and suggests clinicians seek out more inclusive, expanded, and multicultural clinical theory and research to better meet the needs of clients. The case shows how race itself and racial ideology show up for both the client and for the practitioner. Consider how the clinican might have specific dialogue with the client regarding their interactional identity, experince of race, racism, and colorism, and how these experince show up in daily life both socially and systemically. Conversation of race and racism are not a one and done conversation in clinical practice, but rather an intentional aspect of practice that should be considered and utilized across the treatment period. For Donte, race is present in all areas of his socialization (family, church, school, career, and peer relationships) and within all systems he interacts in (armed forces, medicine, policing, education, etc.), and so racism has the likelihood of also holding presence (and power). In Donte's clinical work it was necessary to teach and skill build with Donte the ability to connect his experiences of race and racism to his mental and emotional health and demonstrate how he might combat the experiences when present. The CRT tenet, *racism is endemic*, tells us that racism is ordinary and permanent, and that clinicians are called upon to center this knowledge within tier practice and consider how it might or does show up in a client or family's treatment process and maintenance. For Donte, a significant part of the healing process was understanding how his Black family, his church community, the military (his past employer), and even his current career (medicine), often unintentionally perpetuate race based oppression and how being on the receiving end of this has caused his deep harm and hindered his past insight and clinical treatment. Today, post treatment with our practice, he is able to manage these key aspects of treatment on his own.

Discussion Questions

1. In what ways did the CRT tenet, racism is endemic, manifest itself in the case problem?
2. How do racial and ethnic identity orientations of both the client and the clinician interact in clinical practice?

3. How might you challenge Eurocentric schools of thought, to ensure your approach in the classroom, practicum, or in clinical practice meets the needs of people of color?
4. For students: How might you adapt a CRT lens to your practicum or early career clinical experience? How do you proceed when your practice environment is resistant to utilizing the CRT lens?
5. For clinical supervisors: How might you introduce and embed a CRT lens within your clinical supervision of practicing clinicians and practicum placement students?

REFERENCES

Aymer, S. (2010). Clinical practice with African-American men: What to consider and what to do. *Smith College Studies in Social Work, 80*(1), 20–34.

Bell, D. A. (1995). Who's afraid of critical race theory? *University of Illinois Law Review*, 1995(4), 893–910.

Capps, J. (2020, September 27). Critical Theory Tenets: A Process-Based Guide for Social Work Practice. In S. Chun Wetterau, R. Cordova, J. Capps, & L. Laguitan (Presenters), Critical Race Theory as a Tool to Dismantle Anti-Blackness in API Communities [Workshop Session]. Asian Pacific Islander Social Work Council, NASW-CA, United States.

Currie, N. (2026). *Case studies in decolonized social work supervision.* Cambridge University Press. [Manuscript in preparation].

Centers for Disease Control and Prevention. (2021). The State of the HIV Epidemic. Retrieved on January 21, 2024 from www.cdc.gov/nchhstp/newsroom/fact-sheets/hiv/state-of-the-hiv-epidemic-factsheet.html

Delgado, R., & Stefancic, J. (Eds.). (2013). *Critical race theory: The cutting edge.* Temple University Press.

Kolivoski, K. M., Weaver, A., & Constance-Huggins, M. (2014). Critical race theory: Opportunities for application in social work practice and policy. *Families in Society, 95*(4), 269–276.

Miller, J. L., & Garran, A. M. (2017). *Racism in the United States: Implications for the helping professions.* Springer Publishing Company.

Shaia, W. E. (2019). SHARP: A framework for addressing the contexts of poverty and oppression during service provision in the United States. *Journal of Social Work Values & Ethics, 16*(1), 16–26.

Shaia, W. E., Avruch, D. O., Green, K., & Godsey, G. M. (2019). Socially engineered trauma and a new social work pedagogy: Socioeducation as a critical foundation of social work Practice. *Smith College Studies in Social Work, 89*(3–4), 238–263.

CASE 2.2

Medical Mistrust in the Black Community
Navigating Endemic Racism in Medicine and Child Welfare

EBONY N. PEREZ

This case highlights the CRT tenet of racism is endemic, which purports that racism is tightly woven into all aspects of society and has implications for racial minorities. The case discusses how the endemic nature of race and racism affects Black individuals' level of trust in the medical system.

The medical establishment has a long history of mistreating Black Americans. Medical doctors have historically portrayed Black people as innately diseased, and dehumanized their suffering, using scientific arguments to create an illusion of neutrality and objectivity. In 1851, Southern physician, Samuel Cartwright, described "drapetomania," a so-called mental illness that he claimed caused enslaved Africans to flee captivity; he argued that this could be prevented by keeping Black people in submission and "cured" by whippings.

Similarly, J. Marion Sims, known as the father of modern gynecology, achieved his landmark vesicovaginal fistula repair through repeated surgeries performed without anesthesia on enslaved Black women. In the infamous Tuskegee syphilis study, which ran from 1932 to 1972, researchers withheld treatment from hundreds of Black men to observe the disease's progression. These gruesome atrocities set the stage for creating the foundation of mistrust in the medical community.

Medical mistrust is not only related to past legacies of exploitation but also stems from people's contemporary experiences of discrimination in health care. There are inequities within access to health insurance, health care facilities, and treatments to institutional practices that make it more difficult for Black Americans to obtain care. The United States is one of the most dangerous places in the world for a woman to give birth. In 2022, there were twenty-two maternal deaths for every 100,000 live births in the US, more than double, sometimes triple, the rate for most other high-income countries (Gunja et al., 2024). When comparing maternal mortality and maternity care in the US with ten other high-income countries, Tikkanen et al. (2020) found that the US had the highest maternal mortality rate. In seven of the countries, there were less than five maternal deaths per 100,000 live births, while in the US the rate was seventeen deaths per 100,000 live births (Tikkanen et al., 2020). Research has found Black people receive worse quality care than White people on 53 percent of measures, including measures of care process, such as the ability to receive needed care; care outcomes, such as death; and patients' perceptions of care (NPFW, 2023). Other data show that racial disparities exist both within hospitals and between hospitals for maternal morbidity (Gunja et al., 2024). This bias has life-and-death consequences. Black women are three times more likely to die from pregnancy-related complications than White women (Centers for Disease Control, 2024). Discrimination contributed to 12 percent of pregnancy-related deaths in 2019 (NPWF, 2023). While the statistics have been well documented in the medical community, clinicians still struggle to close the gap and foster trust among families of color. This has led families and reproductive rights activists to establish alternative pathways that focus on centering women of color who have been left out of the conversation.

According to a report released by the National Partnership for Women and Families (NPWF) in 2022, from 2019 to 2020, the largest increase in home births was among Black parents at 30 percent, followed by Indigenous parents at 26 percent, and Latinx parents at 24 percent. The report contributes this increase in alternative birthing choices to the "higher risk of maternal mortality and morbidity they face and the impact of discrimination and structural racism and hospitals that result in lower quality care." Yet, acceptance of inequitable treatment as "normal" is historically rooted in and supported by the belief that Black people are intrinsically disease prone and, implicitly or explicitly, not deserving of high-quality care. Additionally, these beliefs have led to the thinking that Black people are unable to comprehend medical consequences and make informed decisions about their care (Hoffman et al., 2016; McFarling, 2023).

What follows is a case study of a social worker handling a report of medical neglect.

Investigating Medical Neglect

Victoria has worked as a social worker with Children, Youth, and Families Services (CYFS) for ten months. Today she was assigned a new case, the Walker Family. The family's pediatrician made the report concerning an eight-day-old, Black female named Ava. Ava's mother, Tiffany, had a home birth with a midwife and her husband, Jason. This is Victoria's first time investigating a potential case of medical abuse. Per the medical report, Ava was brought in following an uncomplicated at-home birth with a midwife. The family's midwife did a postpartum checkup on mom and Ava within forty-eight hours and another checkup on day three. The family made an appointment with their long-time pediatrician so that "Ava could begin her series of vaccines." During the visit, the pediatrician noticed that Ava had developed jaundice and recommended she be admitted to the hospital for treatment. The report states "jaundice is easily treated in the hospital." After "providing the risk factors and explaining that the hospital would use phototherapy and monitor levels, mom still did not agree." Following that, the doctor reported they told mom to "go home and think about it" but "informed mom they would make arrangements for Ava to be admitted at a local hospital." The parents did not show up at the hospital. Once the hospital notified the doctor that Ava was not admitted, the doctor called CYFS and filed a report of medical neglect.

As a recent graduate, Victoria recalls a project she completed in her macro-social work class and is well aware of the vast disparities in maternal mortality rates among Black women. Victoria recalls focusing on women's access to healthcare in her local area when completing a community needs assessment for one of her class projects. From this project, she learned that there has been an overall increase in people choosing to have home births, with the largest increase being among Black women. Victoria is also well aware of the laws regarding mandated reporting and has carefully reviewed the state definitions of "neglect," recognizing that they are extremely vague and subjective. These definitions often leave significant room for interpretation, which can lead to inconsistent application and outcomes. When a report of medical neglect comes from a doctor, it automatically triggers an investigation by CYFS, adding to the urgency and gravity of the situation.

Realizing that Ava is a two-week-old baby, the timing of meeting with the family will be crucial. She also believes it is important to follow up with the doctor and midwife who delivered and has been caring for Ava and Tiffany. This will provide additional medical information and give her a better idea of how the family has been with meeting Ava's medical needs. Lastly, she also feels it is important to speak directly with the doctor who made the report to hear their concerns beyond what is written.

Victoria begins to work on her case plan for the investigation to determine if Ava is indeed being subjected to medical neglect.

Victoria takes time to note some key observations in the case. Based on the doctor's report that Ava's bilirubin level is high, the interview with the family needs to occur immediately. She feels it is important to confirm and clarify the details of the report for accuracy. She contacted the office to see if the doctor was able to speak either by phone or via virtual meeting. The doctor stated either would work, so Victoria arranged a virtual meeting. The doctor was more than willing to speak with Victoria and shared that the most important thing is to get Ava admitted to the hospital ASAP. The doctor confirmed, "while the bilirubin level is high, it is not critical at this time and is easily treatable in the hospital." They also added that the mother shared that she "felt more comfortable working with their midwife and treating her daughter at home." They shared that the parents were using a "fiber-optic blanket" and "being monitored by the midwife." Several times during the conversation, the doctor made condescending statements about "those people do not typically understand medical advice" and that although they have worked with the family for "several years with their older children and have never had concerns," "they want Ava admitted." When Victoria asked for clarification of "which people" the doctor was referring to, they clarified, "you know, young families." Additionally, the doctor shared they did not "believe the people at the Umoja Pregnancy Center really understand complications during or after birth." Victoria then followed up and asked if jaundice is an unusual occurrence at this time for a newborn, to which they replied that it "occurs in about 60% of infants, and that's why it is so treatable." They also expressed that they "understood the family wants to work with the midwife, however, a midwife treating jaundice at home is not appropriate."

Next, Victoria determines that she will speak with the midwife, Andrea Taylor, before speaking with the family. She also connected with Ms. Taylor via Zoom to discuss her work with the family. Victoria shared that she is gathering information about how the family is treating Ava's jaundice. She learns that the Umoja Pregnancy Center specializes in caring for Black women and girls and their reproductive health. Ms. Taylor also shared she has "provided prenatal care throughout Tiffany's 3 pregnancies and is still providing postpartum care." Ms. Taylor shared she has "been a practicing midwife for 7.5 years and worked with the Walker family for 6 of those years." Ms. Taylor stated that the parents are very loving and caring with three kids under five years old who are dedicated to their kids' physical, emotional, and spiritual health. Victoria asked Ms. Taylor to describe the birthing process for Mrs. Walker. Ms. Taylor revealed that it was a typical labor and delivery with no complications. She shared that it is common for newborns to develop jaundice, particularly when a sibling has had jaundice, and that her older brother's jaundice was successfully treated at home. She also shared that she has been treating Ava's jaundice at home with a carefully curated plan; the Walkers have been following the plan of care, and Ava's condition is improving.

Drawing on principles from Critical Race Theory (CRT), Victoria remains acutely aware of the broader social and racial contexts that influence these interactions. She understands that Black and other marginalized families are often disproportionately targeted and face harsher judgments in child welfare cases. Victoria's goal is to approach the situation with a critical awareness of these dynamics, striving to advocate for the family's rights and well-being within a system that has historically marginalized them.

Victoria understands that these investigations can feel invasive and punitive, often exacerbating the trauma for the families involved. She knows that once an investigation begins, the family's interactions with CYFS workers are meticulously documented. Therefore, she lets them know that every piece of information shared can influence the outcome, potentially leading to findings of neglect based on subjective interpretations rather than clear evidence. To navigate these challenges, Victoria takes a proactive and supportive approach during her home visit. Mrs. Walker answers the door and is understandably surprised and upset by Victoria's visit. After Victoria introduced herself and stated she had "not made any decisions, however, she would like to understand her and her husband's choice." Victoria also explained, "due to a medical neglect report being made, there must be an investigation per the state rules." Victoria stated she would like to come in to hear their side of things.

The family reluctantly allows Victoria to come in to speak with them. Victoria begins by apologizing for having to interrupt this important bonding time for the family with Ava. Mrs. Walker nods uncomfortably as Victoria continues. Victoria states, "I cannot imagine how disruptive this is for you." The Walkers are visibly upset, so Victoria maintains a softer approach. She explains that, unlike the criminal legal system, where individuals have clearly defined rights, families facing an investigation by CYFS do not have the right to counsel or the right to remain silent. She shares, "the lack of procedural protections places families at a distinct disadvantage. Any comments they make, or even their silence, can be used against them in the investigation process." She explains to the family that while they do not have the right to remain silent or the right to counsel, they do have the right to be treated with respect and dignity. She provides them with information about what to expect during the investigation and advises them on how to communicate effectively with CYFS workers. By preparing the family and setting clear expectations, Victoria aims to reduce their anxiety and help them feel more in control of the situation. This reality of being involved in an investigation into neglect or abuse can be particularly daunting and overwhelming for families, especially those from marginalized communities who may already distrust state institutions due to historical and ongoing systemic injustices.

During the interview, Victoria learned that Jason's family moved to the area when he was young and Tiffany remained after college. They met in their sophomore year of school and began dating in their senior year. Tiffany is an accountant, and Jason is an engineer. Jason revealed that his extended family still lives in the area, and they see them at least twice a month. While Tiffany's family does not live in the area, her extended family visits regularly, especially her parents, as their kids are the only grandchildren. Furthermore, both are active in various community and social organizations. They have access to healthcare services and do not have any significant financial stressors. Tiffany revealed that she has always had a midwife since she began gynecological care as a teen. She stated that the only Black female providers in her area were midwives. Moreover, Tiffany is very aware that the maternal mortality rate for Black women is higher in the US. Her desire to have her care supervised by a Black woman and her knowledge of the impact of racial bias on healthcare outcomes is central to the family's approach to medical care in this situation. Jason remarked that he is in full support of his wife, particularly after doing some of his own research on the topic. He also added that their older child had jaundice too and they knew that there was an increased chance Ava might experience it as well. They had a treatment plan developed prior to her birth just in case. They were able to describe in detail the care plan and how they are implementing it. They both shared they have confidence in Ms. Taylor's ability to guide them and let them know if Ava needs more extensive medical intervention.

Before ending the visit, Victoria also emphasizes the importance of documenting their interactions and keeping records of any communications with CYFS. She suggests that the family reach out to community advocates or support groups who can offer guidance and stand with them throughout the process. By doing so, she hopes to empower the family and mitigate the power imbalances inherent in the investigation process.

After meeting with the family, Victoria highlighted the family's strengths and protective factors in her report. For example, although the Walkers decided not to admit Ava to the hospital, they were taking Ava's condition seriously and treating her at home under the guidance of a different yet experienced medical professional. She also notes that the family had been open and cooperative with the process.

In summary, Victoria's knowledge of the vague and subjective nature of neglect definitions, combined with her awareness of the family's lack of rights during CYFS investigations, informs her compassionate and strategic approach. By providing the family with clear information, support, and advocacy resources, she seeks to mitigate the harm and trauma associated with the investigation, aiming to ensure a fairer and more just process for the family involved.

Implications for Practice: So What Does It Mean?

If the endemic nature of race and racism is not considered in this situation, several significant implications for practice may arise. Firstly, there is a heightened risk of misdiagnosis and inappropriate interventions. Without acknowledging systemic racism, biases are more likely to influence the diagnosis and classification of neglect, leading to interventions that do not address a family's needs or mistakenly involves them with the child welfare system. Misunderstanding or misinterpreting the family's behavior and circumstances can result in incorrect assessments and potentially harmful recommendations.

Additionally, failing to consider the impact of racism can severely erode trust between Black families and child welfare agencies. This mistrust can hinder cooperation and communication, making it more difficult to support the family effectively. The relationship between the family and service providers may be damaged, reducing the likelihood that the family will seek help in the future. Moreover, ignoring the role of race and racism can reinforce existing disparities in child welfare and healthcare outcomes. Black families may continue to face disproportionate scrutiny and harsher consequences compared to their white counterparts, perpetuating systemic injustice within the child welfare system and contributing to ongoing cycles of disadvantage and discrimination for marginalized communities.

Interventions that are not culturally sensitive or appropriately tailored to the family's unique context are less likely to be effective. The family may not receive the comprehensive support they need, including access to culturally competent healthcare, mental health services, and community resources. Ethical and legal ramifications also arise from neglecting the impact of systemic factors. Social workers and other professionals have an ethical obligation to consider the influence of racism. Failing to do so can violate professional ethical standards and harm the family, potentially leading to legal challenges against the child welfare agency.

The long-term consequences for the family can be severe. Their mental health and well-being can be adversely affected by an investigation perceived as unfair or biased, potentially causing lasting psychological harm (Dettlaff et al., 2023; Kaplan et al., 2019). The risk of unnecessary removal of children from their homes increases, leading to significant disruption and trauma for the family. To mitigate these implications, practitioners should engage in ongoing training on implicit bias, cultural competence, and the impact of systemic racism. Implementing inclusive policies that explicitly address the role of race and racism in child welfare practices is crucial. Fostering partnerships with community organizations and advocates, striving for greater diversity within child welfare agencies, and establishing mechanisms for accountability and oversight are essential steps to ensure more equitable and just outcomes for all families.

Discussion Questions

1. What examples of the endemic nature of racism do you observe in this case study?
2. How can an understanding of the endemic nature of racism help improve child welfare agencies' practices and policies?
3. In what ways do biases, stereotypes, and microaggressions affect the interactions between CYFS professionals and children and families from racially marginalized communities?
4. How can community engagement and collaboration be leveraged to challenge and change racist structures within CYFS?
5. How can data collection, research, and evaluation be utilized to identify and eliminate racial disparities in CYFS systems?

REFERENCES

Agency for Healthcare Research and Quality. 2018 National Healthcare Quality and Disparities report (AHRQ publication no. 19-0070-EF). Rockville, MD: Department of Health and Human Services, www.ahrq.gov/sites/default/files/wysiwyg/research/findings/nhqrdr/2018qdr-finales.pdf

Centers for Disease Control. (2024, April 8). Working Together to Reduce Black Maternal Mortality. www.cdc.gov/womens-health/features/maternal-mortality.html

Dettlaff, A. J., Abrams, L. S., & Teasley, M. L. (2023). Interrogating the carceral state: Re-envisioning social work's role in systems serving children and youth. *Children and Youth Services Review, 148*. https://doi.org/10.1016/j.childyouth.2023.106920

Gunja, M. Z., Gumas, E. D., Masitha, R., & Zephyrin, L. C. (2024, June 4). Insights into the U.S. Maternal Mortality Crisis: An International Comparison [Issue Briefs]. The Commonwealth Fund.

Hoffman, K. M., Trawalter, S., Axt, J. R., & Oliver, M. N. (2016). Racial bias in pain assessment and treatment recommendations, and false beliefs about biological differences between blacks and whites. *Proc Natl Acad Sci USA, 113*, 4296–4301. https://doi.org/10.1073/pnas.1516047113

Kaplan, K., Brusilovskiy, E., O'Shea, A. M., & Salzer, M. S. (2019). Child protective service disparities and serious mental illnesses: Results from a national survey. *Psychiatric Services, 70*(3), 202–208. https://doi.org/10.1176/appi.ps.201800277

McFarling, U. L. (2023, April 14). In Counties with More Black Doctors, Black People Live Longer, "Astonishing" Study Finds. www.statnews.com/2023/04/14/black-doctors-primary-care-life-expectancy-mortality/

National Partnership for Women & Families. (2023, December). Black Women's Maternal Health: A Multifaceted Approach to Addressing Persistent and Dire Health Inequities. National Partnership for Women & Families: Home Page. Retrieved June 12, 2024, from http://nationalpartnership.org

Simon, J., & Joseph, R. (2023). Teaching intersectionality to enhance MSW students' understanding of oppression and privilege. *Journal of Teaching in Social Work, 43*(4), 432–448. https://doi.org/10.1080/08841233.2023.2244997

Smedley, B. D., Stith, A. Y., & Nelson, A. R. (Eds.). (2003). *Unequal treatment: Confronting racial and ethnic disparities in health care.* National Academies Press.

Tikkanen, R., Gunja, M. Z., FitzGerald, M., & Zephyrin, L. (2020, November 18). Maternal Mortality and Maternity Care in the United States Compared to 10 Other Developed Countries [Issue Briefs]. The Commonwealth Fund.

Washington, H. A. (2006). *Medical apartheid: The dark history of medical experimentation on Black Americans from colonial times to the present.* Doubleday Books.

Willoughby, C. D. (2018). Running away from drapetomania: Samuel A. Cartwright, medicine, and race in the Antebellum South. *J South Hist, 84*, 579-614.

CASE 2.3

Adversity at the Crossroads
Navigating the Challenges of Transgender Homelessness

ASHLEY R. GARRICK

This case involves a transgender African American adult who encounters a housing crisis and experiences homelessness. Issues pertaining to race, gender identity, trauma, and social inclusivity are addressed. A CRT lens of intersectionality is applied to discuss implications for future practice.

Background

Kenyatta is a twenty-seven-year-old first-generation African American who is transitioning from male to female and identifies as a woman. Kenyatta has not completed any gender-affirming surgery but is in the process of petitioning to have her gender markers changed on all legal documents. She does not intend to undergo a name change, as Kenyatta is known in African cultures as a gender-neutral name. She also values the positive meanings associated with her name, one being "jewel." Both of her parents are living; however, they have a strained and distant relationship due to differences in spiritual beliefs and values. Kenyatta is an only child and has little to no interaction with extended family members and minimal meaningful relationships outside of casual dating partners and one close friend named Trinity. Kenyatta lives in a developing small town in a southeastern state where transgender equality laws and policies are not supported.

Family and Childhood

Kenyatta was born into a conservative family in the southeastern states of America after her parents migrated from a small country in Africa. Her parents have strict traditional family values and expectations, so they have not been supportive of her gender expression and recent gender identity transition. They find it impossible to accept Kenyatta's gender identity and expression due to these values not aligning with what they have taught her to believe. Kenyatta was raised to believe that men are expected to marry women, have children, and provide for the family as a leader and head of household. Growing up, Kenyatta felt isolated and emotionally trapped, which resulted in avoidance of close relationships. She has, however, maintained one close friend from her childhood – Trinity. Trinity and Kenyatta have been close friends since elementary school. Throughout her transition, Trinity has been supportive and provides a source of trust and comfort. Kenyatta has been subjected to substantial emotional abuse in her home as well as in grade school due to her non-conforming gender expression. This experience of rejection has left deep emotional scars. At the age of eighteen, Kenyatta found herself torn between what she believed her true identity to be and her family's cultural expectations. She spent her entire life hiding her authentic self but could no longer deny the powerful feeling that she needed to live as her true self, a Black woman. After mustering the courage to speak her truth, she sat down with her family to confess her feelings and desire to live her life as a woman. Her father expressed that she is his only son and if he cannot be that then he must leave. She made the painful decision to leave her family's house, severing ties with her parents.

Education and Employment

Kenyatta earned an associate degree in human services, after participating in a "No Cost" college program that made education accessible to her. Her dreams of living a successful and fulfilling life were put on hold as she faced the harsh realities of discrimination and harassment due to her race and transgender identity. Kenyatta was laid off from her job and the difficulties she encountered in her job search were disheartening. Employers often judged her because she was Black and transgender, making it difficult to secure meaningful employment. She tried to make ends meet by working in low-wage jobs, but the income was far from sufficient to cover her living expenses. Reality set in as Kenyatta realized her unique set of challenges. While most Black Americans experience discrimination based on their race, scholars and activists say the nature of discrimination changes with people who have multiple identities. This intersectionality produces different and, often, worse experiences of inequality. Within the Black community, most Black people believe racial discrimination should be prioritized over other inequalities such as discrimination against LGBTQ+ people (Cox, 2023). Where does this leave Kenyatta as a Black transwoman whose family immigrated to the country? She is facing expectations of gender within the southern Black community where views on gender equality and identity are a core part of religion or a sense of morality – the same as her family she is distanced from.

Kenyatta's financial instability has affected her ability to meet her rent payments, leading her to receive an eviction notice. It marks another challenging chapter in her life, leaving her without a stable place to call home. Adding to the weight of her struggles, she is without any source of income, in addition to cycling through episodes of depression and anxiety. She does not receive any public benefits and is not qualified for state-regulated programs like Medicaid because she does not meet the eligibility requirements, leaving her in an even more vulnerable position. After her experiences with employment, she is hesitant to request benefits out of fear of further discrimination as this is common for transgender women of color when navigating public welfare systems. This proves to be an additional barrier and further exacerbation of racial and gender inequality. It is a daily battle to secure her basic needs and maintain a sense of dignity. The lack of health insurance only adds to her worries, making it difficult to access the healthcare needed as she battles depression and anxiety stemming from the uncertainty of her future and ability to become self-sufficient.

The Downward Spiral

For support, Kenyatta has a connection to an online LGBTQ+ support group that is composed of members of different races, ethnicities, sexual orientations, and gender identities. The purpose of the support group is to acknowledge shared experiences and address the needs of individuals within the community. She has also been able to live with her friend Trinity as she continues her search for employment in the human services field. Her relationship with Trinity has recently become strained over finances and her inability to contribute to household expenses.

After attending a job fair, she returned home to find a twenty-four-hour eviction notice on the front door. When she asked about the eviction notice, Trinity blamed her for not being able to contribute and said if she had a job, none of this would be happening. Not only had the rent increased, but Trinity had also been paying additional expenses for food and other necessities that Kenyatta was unable to provide without any income. She immediately feels crippled by fear after already experiencing one eviction and desperately attempts to discuss options for other living arrangements. Trinity tells Kenyatta that she is moving back with her parents and can no longer help someone who does not seem to want to help themselves.

Kenyatta attempts to connect with her family. However, her father is adamant about her not returning home because she has made her decision and must live with it. She has been unable to secure her own housing due to her recent eviction and experiencing discrimination from homeowners who advertised rooms for rent but were unwilling to accept her as a tenant due to her being Black and transgender. She connects with her LGBTQ+ support group and receives information about local homeless shelter programs. She is extremely overwhelmed and does not know where to begin. She contacts the local domestic violence shelter and is not eligible for services due to not being in immediate danger and is referred to another crisis center. She is able to access an emergency shelter that provides beds on a first-come, first-served basis but she is not able to secure a bed every night, which causes additional stress. She contacts another emergency shelter program where women are offered the opportunity to stay up to ninety days with a secured spot in the program and receive case management and additional support services from a social worker. She schedules an intake appointment over the phone. She is informed that at her intake appointment, she will need to provide a copy of her ID and that a criminal background check must be completed before entering the program. She chooses not to disclose being transgender until she meets with the social worker out of fear of discrimination before she has a chance to advocate for her needs.

Social Work Engagement and Assessment

When Kenyatta arrives for her appointment at the emergency shelter program, she meets Jodie, a Master-level social work practitioner who has been employed with the agency for ten years, and her social work intern, Jessica. She is asked for her consent to have Jessica be a part of the meeting and she agrees. She is then met with a series of intake questions aimed at understanding her needs and circumstances. These questions are crucial in helping the social worker provide the appropriate assistance and support. As the conversation progresses, questions then begin to focus on her gender identity. She openly shares that she identifies as female. However, a noticeable discrepancy arises when the intake worker glances at her identification, which still bears the label of "male." This discrepancy between her gender identity and the gender marker on her ID sparks a pivotal moment in their interaction.

With a compassionate tone, Jodie explains that due to the gender marker on her identification, they will encounter challenges in providing her with housing tailored to her identity. Unfortunately, the immediate housing solution they planned for may not align with her gender identity and they offer a referral to the local men's shelter as the only available option at that moment.

This places Kenyatta in a deeply uncomfortable and distressing position. The thought of being housed in a shelter designated for men triggers concerns about her safety and reminds her of the negative experiences she had during childhood. She has no desire to be housed with individuals whose gender identity differs from her own. She expresses this concern with Jodie and pleads for her to reconsider. Jodie requests additional time to consult with her program director to ensure that she can meet Kenyatta's needs. This will be her first time working with a Black transgender woman and she wants to be able to provide the best care possible. In the meantime, Jodie provides Kenyatta with a hotel voucher for one week.

After Kenyatta leaves the office, Jessica expresses concern regarding Kenyatta's clear anxiety around and discomfort with the prospect of being housed with men due to her gender identity. She recognizes how challenging the situation is to navigate and asks Jodie what she will do. Jodie states that she is not entirely sure, as she has not experienced this type of situation in her time of practice. Jodie mentions working with some Black women in the past, but Kenyatta is different. Jessica begins to reflect on the responsibility of social workers to uphold ethical standards, advocate for fairness and equal treatment, and lessen feelings of marginalization and unsafety. Jodie assures Jessica that she understands the ethical considerations; however, Kenyatta is not currently a client of the agency at this point and is not sure how to proceed in the best way.

Social Work Intervention Using a Lens of Intersectionality

Jessica suggests considering Kenyatta's experiences through the lens of CRT as her concerns about safety and discomfort seem to be deeply rooted in her past experiences, which are shaped by both her race and gender identity. Moreover, CRT focuses on understanding and addressing how race intersects with various aspects of society, including power structures and social institutions. While CRT primarily deals with race, it shows how race intersects with identities, such as gender identity, which is relevant in this case. Jodie agrees that Jessica's point is valid; however, given the lack of legal protection for those who identify as transgender, it is challenging to navigate the situation without clear guidelines, especially when Kenyatta is not an official client. Jessica asks if this can be an opportunity to advocate for more inclusive policies within the agency and community at large as CRT teaches to challenge existing social structures to work towards more equitable solutions.

Implications for Practice

Kenyatta is both a person of a particular race and with a distinct gender identity, and this intersectionality shapes her experiences and concerns. Therefore, CRT prompts us to consider how structural inequalities may contribute to Kenyatta's discomfort. The existing shelter system may not adequately address the unique challenges faced by individuals like Kenyatta at the intersection of race and gender identity. Additionally, CRT encourages challenging and questioning existing structures that may perpetuate oppression and marginalization. In this case, it may involve revisiting and reconsidering how shelters are designed and operated to ensure they consider diverse identities and experiences.

Intersectionality

The concept of intersectionality is recognized by CRT, where multiple aspects of a person's identity intersect and contribute to their experiences of privilege or oppression. In Kenyatta's case, her experience is shaped not only by her race but also by her gender identity and cultural background. By acknowledging the interweaving of race and gender, CRT prompts a deeper understanding of the structures of power and discrimination. It prompts us to explore how societal norms, institutional policies, and cultural expectations converge to create a complex web of privilege and disadvantage. In essence, CRT encourages us to move beyond simplistic analyses of oppression based solely on one aspect of identity. Instead, it invites us to consider how various dimensions of identity converge and interact, offering a more comprehensive understanding of the experiences that shape individuals' navigation throughout a society marked by systemic inequalities. Additionally, examining the intersection of race and gender within the context of homelessness requires exploration through a trauma lens. According to the theory of race trauma, individuals from Black, Indigenous, and other People of Color (BIPOC) communities encounter collective trauma originating from historical racism and discrimination (Comas-Díaz et al., 2019). Those who identify as BIPOC have compounded risks for trauma – both at a systemic level due to their BIPOC status and at an individual level – heightening their susceptibility to interpersonal violence. When these individuals simultaneously face homelessness and have gender expressions outside of cisnormativity, the significance of trauma becomes crucial in comprehending their vulnerability on the streets and the best practices needed to alleviate additional adversity. Kenyatta's plea for housing consideration based on her gender identity serves as an example of the necessity to recognize and respect the unique experiences and needs of individuals who sit at the edges of intersecting marginalized identities, such as being Black and transgendered. Considering intersectionality in practice allows for a shift away from a one-size-fits-all approach to policies and practices. Instead, it calls for an understanding of the diverse challenges faced by different groups and underscores the importance of tailoring solutions to address these specific concerns. Thus, CRT promotes a departure from a singular focus to one that acknowledges the lived realities of intersecting identities. It encourages proactive engagement with the narratives of those who have been historically silenced, enabling a more comprehensive understanding of the multifaceted ways in which structural inequalities manifest.

Structural Inequality

Research has found that rates of homelessness are higher among non-Hispanic Blacks (16.8 percent) and Hispanics of any race (8.1 percent) compared to non-Hispanic Whites (4.8 percent). Even after accounting for factors like education, veteran status, and geographic region, the disparity between Black and White individuals persists, while the gap between Hispanics and Whites loses statistical significance (Fusaro et. al., 2018). When compounded with gender identity, there are additional disparities. So, CRT emphasizes the role of structural inequalities and how existing systems can perpetuate oppression. In this scenario, the existing shelter system might not adequately address the specific needs and concerns of individuals with diverse gender identities. Transgender and non-gender-conforming homelessness is increasing where most transgender adults who become homeless are disproportionately unsheltered and more likely to remain unsheltered than adults who do not identify as transgender. The existing shelter system, often designed with a heteronormative and cisnormativity framework, inadvertently marginalizes transgender individuals, leading to a disproportionate representation of this community among the homeless population.

Jodie's decision to consult with her program director is an opportunity to bring attention to the need for inclusive policies that consider the intersectionality of identities allowing her the opportunity to focus on challenging and transforming existing structures. It is essential to advocate for policies that recognize and address the intersecting identities of individuals, creating a more inclusive and responsive social support system that respects the dignity and safety of everyone, including those with diverse gender identities like Kenyatta. Adopting a culturally responsive approach involves utilizing strength-based, action-oriented methods, and demonstrating respect for all individuals in practice. This approach encompasses honoring dignity, facilitating participation in decision-making, ensuring quality amenities, providing access to social support networks, and allowing individuals to choose their service providers (Bennet & Morse, 2023).

Temporary Solutions

Jodie's prompt provision of a hotel voucher for one week exemplifies a responsive approach to address the urgency of Kenyatta's immediate housing need. This quick action is compassionate, however, it's essential to view this as a temporary solution, prompting a broader and more thorough exploration of the existing shelter system and its inclusivity. This may involve reconsidering the accessibility and cultural competence of existing shelters, ensuring that they are equipped to accommodate people from various backgrounds and with intersecting identities. Jodie's response signals a commitment to not just alleviating the immediate crisis, but also advocating for long-term, sustainable solutions, which might involve engaging with community organizations, policymakers, and advocacy groups to drive systemic changes in how shelters operate and how they can better serve marginalized communities. Jodie's actions may catalyze a broader dialogue on the shortcomings of the current shelter system.

Conclusion

Homelessness is a complex issue influenced by many different factors such as economic hardship and instability, lack of affordable housing, mental health issues, stigma, and discrimination. Black transgender individuals are disproportionately affected by homelessness due to rejection by family, workplace discrimination, and higher rates of mental health challenges. Considering Kenyatta is a first-generation African American, born in the United States to immigrant parents, there are additional expectations set by her family that intersect making her situation unique and challenging. Children of immigrant families often experience appearance pressure where the expectation is to appear successful and do things right. Often, looking good is prioritized over feeling good (Constable, 2022). Additionally, those who identify as transgender often face discrimination and stigma affecting their ability to access housing, health care, and employment. This case underscores the complexities and challenges faced by individuals like Kenyatta. It also highlights the importance of creating more inclusive and supportive systems that can better accommodate and respect the gender identities of all individuals seeking assistance and services. Kenyatta's experience serves as a reminder of the ongoing work needed to ensure that everyone, regardless of their gender identity, can access the support and housing they require while feeling safe and dignified.

Discussion Questions

1. How does the concept of intersectionality help us understand the experiences of transgender individuals facing homelessness, considering factors such as race, gender identity, and economic status?
2. How do stigma and discrimination, particularly towards transgender individuals, impact their ability to access housing, health care, and employment? How might these challenges be exacerbated by the intersection of race and gender identity?
3. Considering the experiences of Black transgender individuals facing family rejection, how does this contribute to increased rates of homelessness for this population?

4. How might racial factors complicate the access to stable employment for transgender individuals?
5. How can intersectionality inform policies aimed at addressing homelessness? What specific policy changes might be necessary to address the racial disparities within the homeless population?
6. From an intersectionality perspective, what are some long-term solutions to address not only the immediate needs of homeless individuals but also the systemic issues that contribute to racial disparities within this population?

REFERENCES

Bennett, B., & Morse, C. (2023). The Continuous Improvement Cultural Responsiveness Tools (CICRT): Creating more culturally responsive social workers. *Australian Social Work, 76*. https://doi.org/10.1080/0312407X.2023.2186255

Coaston, J. (2019). The Intersectionality Wars. *The Highlight by Vox*. Retrieved from: www.vox.com/the-highlight/2019/5/20/18542843/intersectionalityconservatism-law-race-gender-discrimination

Comas-Díaz, L., Nagayama Hall, G., & Neville, H. A. (2019). Racial trauma: Theory, research, and healing: Introduction to the special issue. *American Psychologist, 74(1)*, 1–5. https://doi.org/10.1037/amp0000442

Constable, K. (2022). I Grew Up in an Immigrant Family and Felt the Pressure to Maintain Appearances as a First-Generation African-American. *Business Insider*. Retrieved from: www.businessinsider.com/first-generation-african-american-felt-pressure-to-dothings-right-2022-6

Cox, K. (2023). Black Americans Firmly Support Gender Equality but Are Split on Transgender and Nonbinary Issues. Pew Research Center. www.pewresearch.org/race-ethnicity/2023/02/16/black-americans-firmlysupport-gender-equality-but-are-split-on-transgender-and-nonbinary-issues

Fusaro, V. A., Levy, H. G., & Shaefer, H. L. (2018). Racial and ethnic disparities in lifetime prevalence of homelessness in the United States. *Demography, 55(6)*, 2119–2128.

National Alliance to End Homelessness. (2020, July 24). Transgender Homeless Adults & Unsheltered Homelessness: What the Data Tell Us. National Alliance to End Homelessness. Retrieved from: https://endhomelessness.org/resource/transgenderhomeless-adults-unsheltered-homelessness-what-the-data-tell-us/

CASE 2.4

Where Is My Voice?

ALICIA O. TETTEH

This case highlights the importance of advancing the voice of minoritized individuals in a clinical or mental health setting. It introduces us to a Black woman who had been battling anxiety for a long time. The CRT tenet of advancing the voices of those who are marginalized, acknowledges that the voices of people of color are often stifled, and that they are best positioned to tell their own stories.

Presenting Problem

Racial disparities in the workforce reflect long-standing trends of unequal employment, engagement, and outcomes for people of color (Spindle-Jackson et al., 2023). Jasmine is a Black twenty-nine-year-old, cisgender, heterosexual woman. Since the ninth grade, she has been battling anxiety, and the symptoms have increased since then. Jasmine has people-pleasing behaviors, and she feels anxious when communicating with others. Jasmine believes that a lot of her communication issues stem from her mother and how they communicate with each other. Jasmine finds herself scared to share her feelings with her mother and waiting for her mother's response. Jasmine remembers having to change her ways as a child to fit in, and she can see herself doing the same thing as an adult. Jasmine also has dreams that cause her anxiety, and her heart races at times with these symptoms happening between two to three times a week. Jasmine has low confidence when it comes to making decisions in her life, and she is unsure why.

Jasmine reported that she is scared to show up authentically at work because she fears what others might think of her. She works in a corporate environment that she identifies as a White space. Jasmine stated that she feels like she is facing racism at her job because a coworker, a White transgender woman, can present as her authentic self while Jasmine cannot. Jasmine has expressed that she must be more mindful of how she presents at work because of stereotypes. For example, she has made suggestions to leadership that were dismissed on more than one occasion, and when a colleague made the same suggestion, they were praised. Jasmine does not like how her coworkers treat her. Also, her professional recommendations in group discussions were always heavily criticized by her colleagues. Jasmine stated that although she works in leadership, her coworkers stated that they would not hire someone who had an ethnic name. This comment bothered her because she never viewed her name as ethnic and she felt shame around allowing their comments to upset her. Jasmine reported that it is hard for her to adjust to her new environment due to microaggressions at work, which have affected her own perceptions of herself. In fact, Jasmine stated that she has a promotion opportunity coming up soon, and she feels as if she might not get the promotion. She has expressed thoughts that she must work harder and be better because she is Black in a predominantly white space.

Clinical Assessment and Diagnosis

Critical race theory (CRT) emphasizes questioning the discursive constitution of social structures, including institutional policies and practices, to understand how they represent and reproduce racist relationships of power and oppression (Gray et al., 2023). The addressed tenet of CRT in this case study is advancing the voice of those who are marginalized. Jasmine is seeking help with learning how to create and set boundaries to promote balance in her life as well as how to find her voice. Jasmine stated that she needs to learn how to separate her personal and professional life. In the treatment-planning process, Jasmine will discuss different types of boundaries and explore how to set healthy ones. This is important to Jasmine because she desires to learn how to set boundaries at different stages in life. She will also be courageous about advancing her own voice and telling her truth. Jasmine reported that once she learns how to communicate effectively, she can focus more on the things that will help her to be successful in her life. Jasmine stated that she is also seeking how to manage uncomfortable emotions by growing tolerance to discomfort. Jasmine will learn several new skills to help promote *distress tolerance* in her life. Distress tolerance is the individual capacity to experience aversive emotions without it being an unsurmountable challenge (Arnaudova & Amaro, 2020). Jasmine will also work on how to learn different types of communication styles and use assertive communication in necessary spaces. Jasmine will communicate in an assertive manner and share her needs or wants through dialogue. Jasmine worries about her communication out of fear of being viewed as the "angry Black woman." The angry Black woman trope has penetrated American culture to include the workplace. It characterizes Black women as overbearing, ill-tempered and hostile, often shaping their work experiences. This concept is not new and has been displayed over decades in film, books, and politics (Motro et al., 2021). While anger is a common emotion expressed in the workplace, it gets attributed to the Black woman's personality instead of looking at it as a response to a situation.

Helping Jasmine Heal

To help Jasmine with her presenting problem, several approaches were used. These included liberation psychology, hip-hop psychology, and cognitive writing strategies. Liberation psychology refers to the use of psychological approaches to understand and address oppression among individuals and groups (Rivera & Comas-Díaz, 2020). Interventions connected to liberation psychology are spiritual and psychological with the goal of bringing liberation to families, communities, and societies (Rivera & Comas-Díaz, 2020). The Emotional Liberation Circle was created by the Community Healing Network and Association of Black Psychologists as an intervention to heal and overcome Black inferiority. This is done in a group format to foster collaboration, connection, and community. The intervention highlights value in utilizing voice, storytelling, and narrative therapy to break the silence and shame that may be connected to traumatic experiences. It allows survivors to tell their stories of oppression, discrimination, and stigma. The outcomes include an opportunity to heal from contemporary racism and the acquisition of identity and empowerment. Sharing stories allows understanding of the impact of the trauma, narrates a new story and cultivates community care and self-care (Rivera & Comas-Díaz, 2020).

Hip-hop psychology is another intervention culturally aimed at liberation. Expression, creation, and reception of affirming hip-hop music raises critical consciousness, empowerment, self-expression, and interconnectedness for liberation. Participants would share their stories by way of lyrics, share it with others, and reflect on the narrative of others (Rivera & Comas-Díaz, 2020). It can be done individually but has a richness when done in a group format.

Cognitive writing strategies are another way for marginalized clients to have their voices heard. These are especially helpful if the client is not engaged in therapy and can help target cognitive distortions. The client would write out negative thoughts about themselves and then write evidence that disconfirms it as well as write out an empathic response (Archer, 2021).

Outpatient therapy was also recommended for Jasmine to ensure that her needs were met in a timely manner. Outpatient therapy will allow her to talk about her issues in a safe and comfortable space. It will also help Jasmine build rapport with her therapist and ensure that she is getting the right treatment for her current diagnosis. Using the framework of liberation psychology, in session, Jasmine would be encouraged to turn inward and explore not only critiquing herself for what she did wrong but also how race may cause her to experience similar interactions in the future (Abe, 2020). This encouragement of critical consciousness will challenge her to remain introspective and view experiences as a form of liberation in that she is now increasingly aware of the environment she is in and how she can position herself to move accordingly. Such environments include those marred by race. According to CRT's tenet, race and racism are endemic and therefore are pervasive in all environments. Additionally, the exposure to hip-hop music in session, hip-hop psychology, has been identified as a pathway to mobilize in a way that encourages emotion-focused coping or problem-focused coping (Howard, 2024). This could look like having Jasmine identify a song that connects with the emotions she feels about the incidents at work. The music could be used as an opportunity for her voice to feel heard. This approach is consistent with the CRT tenet of advancing the voices of those who are marginalized. A cognitive strategy that a clinician could engage Jasmine in is externalizing the problem. This narrative approach will help her to create distance between her identity and the problem story (Batrouney, 2019). It also makes it possible to connect problems to more systemic issues that may be present, as opposed to placing blame on the individual themselves. This is consistent with the nature of CRT drawing attention to the role of race and racism in shaping individual experiences through such mechanisms as the negative social construction of Black people, the endemic nature of racism, and white privilege.

Implications for Practice

Advancing the voice of those who are marginalized, a tenet of CRT, encourages individuals to have the opportunity to be heard and validated in their experiences. It challenges us to engage in critical inquiry around the impact of systemic racism and power dynamics on the day-to-day functioning of individuals. Although CRT initially was created to prepare law students to interrogate race in society, it has been adopted by social workers as a framework that guides practice, policy, and research. This theory pushes clinicians to be aware of the possible limits of their own perspectives and to keep cultural humility at the forefront of practice. As agents of change who are centered on social justice, it is imperative to not just advance the voices of clients, but to amplify the opportunity for marginalized persons to experience validation through social justice.

Discussion Questions

1. How was Jasmine's voice or lived experience silenced or invalidated in the case?
2. What kind of support can be offered to clients when their concerns have to do with social identities that cannot be altered?
3. What is the impact on our image of self when others have a negative perspective regarding a collective of people?
4. If you were interning or working in an office setting and you observed unfair treatment occurring toward a client, how would you respond?
5. Consider which of the above interventions you could integrate into your current place of work or internship that would advance the voices of those marginalized.

REFERENCES

Abe, J. (2020). Beyond cultural competence, toward social transformation: Liberation psychologies and the practice of cultural humility. *Journal of Social Work Education,* 56(4), 696–707.

Archer, D. (2021). *Anti-racist psychotherapy: Confronting systemic racism and healing racial trauma.* David Archer, Each One Teach One Publications.

Arnaudova, I., & Amaro, H. (2020). Acting with awareness and distress tolerance related to PTSD symptoms among women with substance use disorder. *Mindfulness, 11*, 1460–1468. https://doi.org/10.1007/s12671-020-01362-1

Balaghi, D., & Okoroji, C. (2023). Using critical race theory to support Black students in schools: A call to educators. *International Journal of School & Educational Psychology, 11*(3), 286–297. https://doi.org/10.1080/21683603.2023.2190184

Branco, S. F., & Jones, C. T. (2021). Supporting black, indigenous, and people of color counselors: Considerations for counselor skills training and practice. *Journal of Mental Health Counseling, 43*(4), 281–300.

Busey, C. L., Duncan, K. E., & Dowie-Chin, T. (2023). Critical what what? A theoretical systematic review of 15 years of Critical Race Theory research in social studies education, 2004–2019. *Review of Educational Research, 93*(3), 412–453. https://doi.org/10.3102/00346543221105551

Bussey, S. R., Thompson, M. X., & Poliandro, E. (2022). Leading the charge in addressing racism and bias: Implications for social work training practice. *Social Work Education, 41*(5). https://doi.org/10.1080/02615479.2021.1903414

Gray, A., Blackman-Richards, N., & Rodgers, S. T. (2023). The Experiences of Black Women Diversity Practitioners in Historically White Institutions. https://doi.org/10.4018/978-1-6684-3564-9.ch013

Howard, S. (2024). "Fuck tha police": "Conscious" hip-hop increases Black people's group-based anger and collective action intentions. *Cultural Diversity and Ethnic Minority Psychology*, May 16, 2024.

Kalemba, J. (2023). Migrant black African youths' experiences of racial microaggressions in the workplace. *Sociology, 57*(4), 811–826. https://doi.org/10.1177/00380385221117351

Motro, D., Evans, J. B., Ellis, A. P. J., & Benson, L., III (2021, April 1). Race and reactions to women's expressions of anger at work: Examining the effects of the "angry Black woman" stereotype. *Journal of Applied Psychology, 107*(1), 142–152. http://dx.doi.org/10.1037/apl0000884

Rivera, E. T., & Comas-Díaz, L. (Eds.). (2020). *Liberation psychology: Theory, method, practice, and social justice*. American Psychological Association. https://doi.org/10.1037/0000198-000

Spindle-Jackson, A., Kuykendall, S., Ramirez, M., & Collins, M. E. (2023). Centering race equity within youth workforce development: Utilizing critical race theory. *Community, Work & Family, 20*(2). https://doi.org/10.1080/13668803.2023.2211222

PART III

Case Studies in
Mezzo-Level Practice

CASE 3.1

White Privilege at the Work Opportunity Center

MONIQUE A. CONSTANCE-HUGGINS

This case demonstrates how white privilege penetrates the welfare system in unsuspecting ways. Public assistance programs, like Temporary Assistance for Needy Families (TANF), play an important role in helping families face economic crises. However, the way these programs are implemented can block already vulnerable populations from getting the help they need. According to Critical Race Theory (CRT), whiteness can convey advantages for White individuals and conversely perpetuate burdens for people of color on welfare.

Work Opportunity Center

Work Opportunity Center (WOC) is a welfare-to-work agency in a diverse and bustling city in the US. It is a for-profit organization, which specializes in job placement for individuals on public assistance programs such as TANF. Commonly referred to as welfare, TANF is the primary cash assistance program in the US. In addition, WOC provides individuals with job readiness training on interviewing, writing a resume, and developing soft skills and specialized job skills. Their mission is to help welfare recipients become self-sufficient and therefore less as well as dependent on welfare.

Moreover, WOC works closely with the state's Department of Human Services (DHS) to help identify people who are non-compliant with their TANF work requirement and are therefore at risk of being sanctioned. Additionally, TANF recipients are required to work for twenty hours a week (if the child is under six years) or thirty hours a week (if the child is older) (Center on Budget and Policy Priorities, 2022). A failure to comply with the state work requirement without "good cause," can result in sanctions. A sanction could range from a reduction in benefits to a "full-family" sanction, where the entire family is cut from public assistance. Currently, only five states and Washington DC do not implement a "full-family" sanction. "Good cause" is loosely defined, but could include situations such as not having childcare, being ill, having to care for a sick family member, or not having transportation, among others.

The Problem

The welfare participants at WOC come from diverse racial backgrounds. About 60 percent of the participants are White and 40 percent are people of color. Despite accounting for a minority of the participants in the program, Black welfare recipients make up the majority (70 percent) of those who are sanctioned from it. This means that many Black parents lose crucial support that they need to help their families through economically tumultuous times. The median monthly TANF check is $498 (Thompson et al., 2023), which means it does not cover all of the recipients' basic needs. Nevertheless, it plays an important role in helping families to weather economic storms. Hence, being sanctioned could be devastating for families. What is also devastating for many of the Black families receiving this assistance is what appears to be the inconsistency in which sanctions are administered. This reality has been making many participants very disgruntled. This was the case with Kenrick.

Kenrick

Kenrick was a twenty-six-year-old African-American single man with two daughters, ages nine and seven. He had sole custody of the girls after their mother started abusing drugs and could no longer care for them. Kenrick started receiving TANF after he lost his job as a chef at a local Black-owned restaurant. A fire had broken out in the kitchen and had destroyed the entire restaurant. Kenrick was able to collect unemployment for twenty weeks, but had exhausted his unemployment benefits without being able to find a new job. With no income, and nothing in his savings account, he decided to apply for TANF. At first, Kenrick was hesitant to apply for public assistance given the stigma associated with the program. Most of the individuals he knew on welfare were women. He did not think that being on welfare was "cool" for a man, and he felt like a failure. In fact, he did not want his "buddies" to know that he was on welfare. Once Kenrick's application was approved, he started attending classes at WOC to help with job readiness and placement. Kenrick, however, had several barriers to employment that hindered his ability to meet his mandatory thirty hours of work activity each week. Specifically, Kenrick had a sick mother who lived with him that he needed to care for. As the only child, Kenrick had the sole responsibility of caring for his mother while also having to care for his two children. He was part of a "sandwich generation" – having to care for his parent and children at the same time. This situation of a "sandwich generation" had placed a lot of strain on Kenrick. He often had to leave work early to take his mother to the doctor or get his children from the school bus, when his neighbor was unavailable to help. This situation put a physical strain on him. Specifically, it often caused his blood pressure to spike, which resulted in him having to miss days from work. Further, Kenrick felt that he was denied several jobs because of his identity as a Black man. While Kenrick had to deal with these personal matters, he also had to navigate exchanges with his case manager, Gracelyn.

During Kenrick's first encounter with Gracelyn at WOC, he felt that she was treating him with suspicion. She questioned him a great deal about the circumstances that led to him being on welfare. This made Kenrick feel like he was undeserving of public assistance. Now that Kenrick was having a difficult time meeting his required work hours, Gracelyn was even more suspicious. She did not believe his narrative of having to care for a sick mother and having high blood pressure. "I don't believe that your failure to show up for work counts as good cause," she told a frustrated Kenrick. "As such, I recommended you for full-family sanction." This meant that Kenrick and his children would lose all their TANF benefits.

Kenrick believed that harmful narratives about Black men being aggressive, dishonest, and lazy made it more difficult for Gracelyn to believe him and that ultimately led to the extreme sanction. In fact, he overheard her saying something like "they keep having children, and are abusing public aid." Kenrick was not exactly sure who Gracelyn was referring to, but based on the way he was treated, he believed she was referring to him. Kenrick was not the only one at WOC who was unable to complete his work requirement. Several White women fell short of their required hours, and Kenrick learnt that they either received a less severe sanction, such as a reduction in TANF (not a full sanction like him) or were not sanctioned at all. The latter was the case for Lynn, a thirty-three-year-old White TANF recipient. Lynn and Kenrick started on welfare at the same time. He deduced that their skin color was affording them different experiences on public assistance. For example, from the beginning, the story Lynn gave them for needing cash assistance was embraced and received little-to-no suspicion compared to Kenrick's story. She was viewed as a more credible individual and hence more deserving of welfare dollars. Furthermore, when Lynn failed to meet her required twenty hours of work per week, the officers believed the reason she provided. Accordingly, her failure to meet the hours was termed as "good cause," and she was not sanctioned. Kenrick learnt all of this from Lynn.

Kenrick had heard of the concept of white privilege before. It refers to the advantages that White individuals enjoy because of their skin color (McIntosh, 1989). He knew that his skin color did not give him privilege, but burdens or disadvantages. In fact, Kenrick had experienced being followed closely in a store while shopping for clothes for his two daughters. He was not the only person in the store, but appeared to have been the only person being constantly asked "may I help you," by the store clerk. He did not have the privilege of being seen as an honest shopper. Shopping is one thing, but Kenrick never expected white privilege to show up in a welfare program. He was not the only one, however, noticing the manifestation of white privilege in welfare; Carlos did, too.

New Compliance Manager

Carlos, a Licensed Master Social Worker (LMSW) was recently hired at WOC to lead their compliance unit. This unit was responsible for monitoring work requirements and applying sanctions. During Carlos' first week at the organization, he started reviewing the sanctioning reports and noticed a disturbing trend – the disproportionate rate at which Black TANF recipients were sanctioned compared to their White counterparts. Unfortunately, what Carlos observed was not unique to WOC. Racial and ethnic comparisons of sanctioning rates across the country have revealed that Black families are sanctioned more frequently and harshly than White families (Center on Budget and Policy Priorities, 2022). "Is it that Black individuals are by nature just less compliant to the welfare requirements?" Carlos asked himself. To get a sense of what was driving the numbers, he decided to hold a focus group with Black welfare recipients to get a deeper understanding of their lived experiences on welfare. Themes of being harshly judged and viewed as undeserving and dishonest emerged from the conversations.

To triangulate the data, Carlos decided to interview some of the workers. Many were offended that of all the issues Carlos could choose to focus on in his first month at WOC, he chose the sanctioning rate. They felt that the increasing number of people on welfare was a bigger and more important issue to address. Most workers noted that they were just doing their jobs in documenting work hours and making recommendations for sanctions, and that is just the way the data played out. "If people refuse to work, they will be cut off. This is not an entitlement program," one worker said. "The same rule is applied to everyone," she added. They shunned the idea that Carlos was implying that race was playing a role in the disparity, despite the stark color-coded differences in sanctioning rates.

Carlos believed, however, that while they were "just doing their jobs," the participants had different experiences based on skin color. He remembered learning in his MSW program that skin color affords material benefits to some individuals and burdens on others. Specifically, White welfare recipients have the privilege of being viewed as "deserving poor." This means there is an assumption that their poverty status is not the result of moral failing. Accordingly, they are seen as more deserving of receiving public assistance (Kiebler & Stewart, 2023). Further, they are less likely to be seen as abusers of the welfare system. Meanwhile, Black welfare recipients have the burden of being seen as "undeserving poor." This means they are presumed to have brought poverty on themselves due to their moral deficits and therefore do not deserve assistance. Consequently, they are more likely to be seen as perpetrators of welfare abuse. Carlos realized that the same diminished view of Black individuals that impact them in the job market, is the same diminished view that can affect their experience on welfare. While on welfare, they may be sanctioned unfairly for things outside of their control. It seemed inescapable.

To help the workers become aware of white privilege, and how it manifests itself in their work, Carlos decided to invite an expert, knowledgeable in CRT, to conduct diversity trainings. Unlike previous trainings that the organization held, these trainings did not simply discuss diverse populations, but highlighted the oppression that diverse groups face. The training raised awareness of all types of privilege based on different identities but emphasized white privilege. It explained how race confers material benefits and burdens, and how Whiteness increases the value of one's reputation. According to McIntosh (1989), this privilege gives White individuals social, cultural, and economic privileges. Carlos felt that an understanding of this could play a role in how Black participants are viewed and, ultimately, how sanctions are applied. He also felt the trainings should highlight the barriers to employment, including discrimination that Black individuals face. Following the series of workshops, agency staff started developing critical consciousness of their attitudes towards all welfare recipients and were mindful of how they were engaging with Black recipients and evaluating their participation in work activity. Over the next couple of months, there was a noticeable shift in the sanctioning rate among Black welfare recipients. There was still room for growth, but at least the workers were now centering race in their work. In a follow-up focus group with the welfare recipients, they noted improvement in their relationship with agency staff. Carlos was pleased with the progress but realized that there was still a long way to go.

Implications

Public assistance programs, like TANF, play an important role in helping families face economic crises. Yet, how these programs are implemented can block already vulnerable populations from getting the help they need. White privilege is a CRT tenet that can impact the experiences of welfare recipients. According to CRT, Whiteness can perpetuate advantages for White individuals and conversely convey burdens for people of color. Understanding white privilege can help workers to understand some of the unique reasons why individuals end up on public assistance in the first place. For example, they might be the last ones to get hired and the first ones to be fired based on stereotypes associated with their skin color. They bear the burden of being seen as less employable than their White counterparts. This therefore makes them more susceptible to being on welfare. White privilege, as a phenomenon, can also help workers to understand the challenges recipients may face while on welfare. These same barriers to employment can hinder them from meeting their work requirements. Further, if they are more likely to be seen as abusers of the public assistance, welfare workers would be more inclined to sanction them and to do so severely. Unless workers are aware of the tremendous burdens that Black welfare recipients bear because of their skin color, they will continue to apply sanctioning rules in a biased way and will be less empathetic to their needs and concerns. This results in Black families being disconnected from both work and welfare. This increases their vulnerability to more negative economic conditions such as housing insecurity and eviction (Azevedo-McCaffrey & Aguas, 2024). If we, as a country, are truly serious about providing a safety net for individuals, then we should be aware of phenomena such as white privilege, which poke huge holes in these nets. This will ultimately benefit all Americans. According to Opoku-Agyeman (2020), "if we make the economy better for those who are suffering most, it stands to reason that those efforts would safeguard everyone else, too."

Discussion Questions

1. In what ways does white privilege manifest itself in the case?
2. In addition to the trainings, what else would you recommend for the organization?
3. What examples of white privilege do you see in your practicum or place of employment?
4. How can the lack of privilege affect Black clients at your practicum or place of employment?

REFERENCES

Azevedo-McCaffrey, D., & Aguas, T. (2024). Continued Increases in TANF Benefit Levels Are Critical to Helping Families Meet Their Needs and Thrive. Center on Budget and Policy Priorities. www.cbpp.org/research/income-security/continued-increases-in-tanf-benefit-levels-are-critical-to-helping

Center on Budget and Policy Priorities. (2022). Policy Basics: Temporary Assistance for Needy Families. www.cbpp.org/research/family-income-support/policy-basics-an-introduction-to-tanf

Kiebler, J. M., & Stewart, A. J. (2023). Their great shame is poverty: Women portrayed as among the "undeserving poor" are seen as deserving sexual assault. *Sex Roles, 89*, 236–256.

McIntosh, P. (1989, July/August). White privilege: Unpacking the invisible knapsack. *Peace and Freedom,* 10–12.

Opoku-Agyeman, A. G. (2020). Black Women Best: Economics as a Diversity Problem, and Here's How It Affects Everyone. The Financial Diet. https://thefinancialdiet.com/black-women-best-economics-has-a-diversity-problem-and-heres-how-it-affects-everyone/

Thompson, G. A., Azevedo-McCaffrey, D., & Carr, D. (2023, February). Increases in TANF Cash Benefit Levels Are Critical to Help Families Meet Rising Costs. Center on Budget and Policy Priorities. www.cbpp.org/research/income-security/increases-in-tanf-cash-benefit-levels-are-critical-to-help-families-meet-0

CASE 3.2

You Got What? Liberalism in a Community-Based Agency

NICOLE E. VAZQUEZ

The Situation

Adelante is a relatively small community-based mental health agency with about thirty employees (therapists, case managers, and community outreach workers) set in a predominantly Latinx neighborhood within Los Angeles that explicitly advances social justice in their mission and work. The racial/ethnic makeup of the staff is approximately 60 percent Latinx; 10 percent Black/African American; 5 percent Asian American/Pacific Islander; and 25 percent white,[1] with 90 percent of the leadership positions being held by white individuals, and the other 10 percent by Latinx individuals. Not only does the agency provide low-cost, sliding-scale mental health services, but they are active in the community and often hold "good neighbor" events in the neighborhood, offering food, entertainment, and activities for all community members.

For the last six years, Adelante has offered a twelve-week workshop series called *We Got Y'all* for "at-risk" youth that includes topics such as anger management, healthy relationships, and becoming independent. One of the main components of the series is an emphasis on participants journaling their experience throughout the twelve weeks. For the anger management and healthy relationships modules, the self-reflection prompts encourage participants to journal their triggers that can spur a dangerous and/or violent outburst, focusing on personal behavior and encouraging the individual to take responsibility for wrongdoing. Each series includes approximately thirty participants and the series is offered four times a year, therefore serving approximately 120 youth per year. The series follows an "evidence-based modality" that is on the approved list of modalities from the County Department of Mental Health (DMH), one of Adelante's funders. There are County-approved pre- and post-tests completed just before the start and immediately after completion of *We Got Y'all*. The post-tests consistently show improvement in anger-coping skills, independent behavior, and healthier attitudes regarding relationships. The series is co-facilitated by a bachelor's-level social work case manager and a community outreach worker who is a high school graduate, who are both Latinx, and a therapist who has their Master of Social Work, who is white.

Recently, the co-facilitation team (Team) sent a proposal to the program director, who is white, suggesting a rebranding of *We Got Y'all* that includes shifting the topics from independence to using group dialogue, community building, and community support when addressing anger management and healthy relationships. They also suggested broadening the journaling activity to include role plays and audio/visual recordings so as to incorporate other means of learning, sharing, and recording feelings, experiences, and history. It would also include the integration of indigenous rituals and practices that include sage-burning (smudging), dance, and communal practices in problem solving and accountability when harm occurs.

The rebrand would lengthen the program to at least six months and would be framed as community health dialogues, with the post-tests being offered immediately after, and again six months after the end of the series. The model would shift from staff-led to a less-structured, organic, flatter power structure in which decision-making would be a communal process. Further, the number of participants would be reduced by half, to about fifteen per series, leading to approximately thirty youth served in one year.

After a week of no response from the program director, the Team followed up requesting an in-person meeting with the director. The director replied that same day denying the request, stating "there's nothing wrong with what we've always done; on the contrary, our post-tests show positive results, plus you're wanting to reduce the number of youth served by 25%!" The director also said that indigenous practices are not standardized or evidence-based, that six months is too long to show results, and that the agency's funders would not support long-term "alternative activities," especially when it would decrease the number of youth served. When the Team shares their challenge with their co-workers, they're told to leave things as-is, stating: "don't rock the boat," and "don't make trouble for us."

Critique of Liberalism

We are going to employ the *critique of liberalism* tenet to analyze the Team's challenge and then to break down how to effectively address it.

One aspect of the United States' form of liberalism sits within this country's founding document. The Declaration of Independence's "all Men are created equal" assertion (not to minimize the fact that the framers meant white, land-owning men *only* when stating "Men") follows a value system and thus connotes a belief that we are all born with equal opportunities and onto equal playing fields, thus if we work hard enough and pull ourselves up by our bootstraps, then we will succeed in life. In turn, if we fall on hardship, then it is our fault. Therefore, CRT critiques the idea of liberalism, which not only places responsibility on the individual, but also values objectivity (Razack & Jeffery, 2002) and colorblindness (Delgado and Stefancic, 2001), more appropriately termed color-evasiveness. Liberalism's value system has thus been ingrained in the fabric of our society for centuries and permeates all aspects of our society; social work is not immune. For example, social work largely follows the medical model, which focuses on the individual for the locus of both harm and healing. We then look solely to the individual for treatment, siloing us away from community and failing to look at the larger systems that greatly impact one's life outcomes.

Next, we will analyze how liberalism plays out in our case study, which will be followed by a strategy that centers on an understanding of the impacts of larger systems of power, and leans into communal ways of knowing, being, sharing, and learning.

What Liberalism Looks Like in This Context

Liberalism's values and practices have been ingrained in the fabric of United States' society since even before the Declaration of Independence, starting with the settler colonials in the early 1600s. For centuries since then, these values have manifested in US culture through a set of overt practices, informal and formal policies, and ways of being, along with implicit and explicit expectations of behavior. In 1999, Tema Okun documented the repeated patterns of being and behavior she encountered during her many years of engaging in racial equity work, which she outlines as White Supremacy Culture (WSC) Characteristics (2021). These Characteristics provide an excellent framework for understanding how liberalism plays out in everyday life. *We Got Y'all*'s format, how management responded to the proposed update, and how the Team's colleagues also reacted, display WSC Characteristics in the following ways.

Fear of Open Conflict

The program director avoided sharing bad news with the Team for a week, then rather than meet in person as offered, avoided a potentially uncomfortable conversation by choosing to reply via email, thus attempting to end the discussion. The Team's colleagues urged them not to "rock the boat" or "make trouble," further trying to avoid conflict.

Sense of Urgency

This is the part of our culture in which we need to see immediate results and have little patience for stopping, slowing down, and learning from the process itself. Knowing this characteristic helps us understand the program director shutting down the idea of lengthening the series from twelve weeks to at least six months, and not seeing the benefit of conducting the post-test six months after completion. We have to see results right away!

Objectivity, Worship of the Written Word

We Got Y'all's programming is legitimized as an "evidence-based practice" by research that is ostensibly *objective* and published by use of the *written word* in academic journals. For these reasons, the program is then standardized by powerful funding sources, therefore deeming it an effective practice. Modalities used by nonprofits often come from an approved list that is disseminated by the funder, who is often a public entity, such as DMH in this case. These modalities are seen as objective because they come from research, then become standardized and normalized; therefore, any other modality that is not on the approved list is not viewed as legitimate and is dismissed. Also, the use of journaling as a central feature of *We Got Y'all*, places importance on this practice while negating the benefits of employing other forms of expression such as the spoken word, music, and dance.

Paternalism, Power Hoarding, One Right Way

We see *paternalism* and *power hoarding* play out in three ways: 1) by the program director being the deciding factor in whether the rebrand goes through or not; 2) by the County DMH holding the power as the decision-making authority on funding and holding a narrow list of approved modalities, also furthering the idea of *Only One Right Way*; and 3) we can recognize the power dynamics in this scenario, given that the proposal for indigenous activities was offered by "lower-level" staff, and the decision was in the hands of one person: the program director.

Individualism

Topics such as "becoming independent" emphasizes one of liberalism's main values: individualism. Becoming independent and being your own person is a measure of success in our society, which in and of itself is not necessarily a negative, however an adult living in a multi-generational household that offers communal living and support is looked down upon. Also, the main activity of journaling focuses on an individual and introspective practice, which can be positive; however, it can also serve to isolate and place the responsibility of self-improvement on the individual. In both examples, placing the sole responsibility on the individual misses an opportunity to lean into mutual support and accountability systems so that people do not feel alone and isolated in addressing their challenges.

Quantity over Quality, Progress Is Bigger and More

White Supremacy Culture is impressed by large numbers, as they have come to identify progress and success, producing terms like "bigger is better." Thus, serving 120 youth per year versus thirty is the preferred option. This belief system is reinforced when funders encourage and respond to large numbers of clients served. We have to look to the long-term effectiveness of our actual impact and assess whether we are creating or activating long-term change when we choose to go a mile wide and inch deep versus a mile deep and inch wide (brown, 2017).

Color-Evasiveness

Though not one of Tema Okun's (2021) WSC Characteristics, the idea that "I don't see color," that equality and justice are "colorblind," and that race and ethnicity should not be taken into account when advancing justice are key aspects of United States liberalism. This fallacy is what causes powerful entities such as DMH to take a one-size-fits-all approach when deciding on a modality that most often was tested only in one community with a specific population, then is expected to be replicated effectively in all communities and populations.

Understanding how these examples of liberalism manifest themselves both personally and professionally through everyday practices can provide a foundation to strategize for change and should not be used to openly criticize or target individuals or organizations. They should be used as a tool to understand the status quo, so that we can center marginalized voices, perspectives, and experiences to be more effective in our work. For example, the Team recognized that *everyone* plays into WSC, regardless of their markers of identity. This helped them to understand why their colleagues, who are majority people of color, urged them not to "rock the boat" or "make trouble." Knowing this, helps to not demonize, judge, or look down upon colleagues for following the status quo.

Strategy

The Team members fully believed at their core that a rebranding was necessary and would be more effective for their youth, so they came together and decided on a multi-pronged strategy to change the program director's mind. Their strategy employed their knowledge of the WSC Characteristics (2021), and they used them to their advantage to prove the efficacy of their recommended methods and flip the dominant narrative used to legitimize *We Got Y'all*'s format.

Leaning into the *worship of the written word,* the Team did research of their own and found that the twelve-week, evidence-based modality was based on a study that was conducted only once in the Midwest part of the country with youth who were 85 percent white. The modality therefore was not replicated at all, much less within a large city like Los Angeles that includes Adelante's community, which is comprised mostly of Latinx families. They conducted additional research and provided studies that show the benefits of learning about one's history, tapping into indigenous practices (Garrett et al., 2011; Lopresti, 2017), and drawing on the power of communal strength and support, which pushes back on liberalism's focus on the individual.

They further used the power of the written word to 1) re-issue *We Got Y'all*'s post-test to its twelve-week participants who were six months out of the program, and 2) also employed CRT's *counter-narrative* tenet to center and uplift youth voices by conducting an anonymous survey of all Adelante's youth members to learn what their interests were and what type of programming they feel would best serve them. The positive results of the post-test conducted immediately after the twelve-week series did not hold six months post-series.

Finally, the Team also looked to their organization's bottom line and pointed out that by purchasing 25 percent less journals and feeding 25 percent less youth during the sessions, they would save Adelante money. This tactic coupled with offering it once as a pilot project convinced the program director to give them a chance.

Outcome

After facilitating *We Got Y'all*'s rebrand, the Team administered a post-survey immediately after the end of the series and at six months post-series. Unlike the twelve-session series, the positive results that showed improvement in anger-coping skills, independent behavior, and healthier attitudes regarding relationships yielded in the immediate post-survey held at a significant level even six months after. Further, the comments section of the survey demonstrated that a majority of participants were not only recognizing changes in their own individual behavior but articulated a strengthened feeling of community with their co-participants and the larger community. They attributed these feelings to the indigenous practices incorporated into the series. They also shared that dialoguing in community highlighted common struggles and identified the connection between personal struggles and larger systemic and political issues (e.g., the challenges of finding a job being related to high unemployment rates in their neighborhood in general, which can be attributed to a shortage of well-paid jobs). Participants countered *worship of the written word* in two ways: 1) by creating a video that highlighted issues of concern to their community, and 2) they outreached to neighbors of all ages and organized an open mic night to showcase local talent and bring diverse voices and perspectives together. With the flattening of hierarchies and a shift to a democratic decision-making process, the decision to hold an open mic night was discussed and decided upon in equal parts by the youth and the facilitation Team.

The modeling of communal decision-making had a trickle-up effect within the organization, such that future decision-making for large projects or shifts such as *We Got Y'all*'s transformation was conducted through a democratic voting process, so the power did not fall on the shoulders of only one person.

Finally, the youth and Team collectively came up with a name change for the series: *We Got Each Other*.

Implications for Practice

This case study was drawn from personal experience as someone who has worked in community-based nonprofits, and as a consultant who works with different organizations and has witnessed how liberalism plays out in these settings. The social worker was purposefully kept away from the main focus of the case study to highlight a challenge to WSC by flattening hierarchies and drawing on the strengths of all Team members as one unit working together.

It was purposeful to state that Adelante was explicit about social justice, had a racially and ethnically diverse staff, and actively outreached to the community prior to sharing the program manager's reluctance to support more culturally relevant programming. This was to highlight a phenomenon in which well-meaning entities engage in helpful practices and can also benefit from a deep self-analysis to explore if they are fully and meaningfully addressing their community's needs.

My challenge to the reader when you find yourself in a difficult situation is to identify where and how liberalism is playing out in the scenario, and how you can challenge liberalism by centering marginalized and minoritized people, voices, and experiences. You can ask yourself: upon whose standards are these decisions being made? Is the alternative being negated because it does not fit the mainstream, and will it be more beneficial for the community with which I'm working? The beauty of CRT is that it not only provides us with the language for experiences we have had and for "how things have always been," but also sets a foundation for an effective strategy for transformation.

Discussion Questions

1. Dismissing the effectiveness of indigenous practices because they are not "evidence-based" demonstrates implicit bias. What other examples of implicit bias can you identify from this scenario?
2. Are there other examples of WSC Characteristics that you can identify in this case?
3. Identify three ways that liberalism plays out in your social work program or any agency that you are a part of.
4. What aspects of the scenario do you not agree with, and why?

Note

1 I follow Kimberlé Crenshaw's (1991) reasoning for not capitalizing white, as "white" does not identify a specific cultural group, and is therefore not a proper noun.

REFERENCES

brown, a. (2017). *Emergent strategy*. AK Press.

Crenshaw, K. (1991). Mapping the margins: Intersectionality, identity politics, and violence against women of color. *Stanford Law Review, 43*(6), 1241–1299. https://doi.org/10.2307/1229039

Delgado, R., & Stefancic, J. (2001). Introduction. In R. Delgado & J. Stefancic (Eds.), *Critical race theory: An introduction* (2nd ed.) (pp. 1–17). NYU Press.

Garrett, M. T., Torres-Rivera, E., Brubaker, M., Agahe Portman, T. A., Brotherton, D., West-Olatunji, C., Conwill, W., & Grayshield, L. (2011). Crying for a vision: The Native American sweat lodge ceremony as therapeutic intervention. *Journal of Counseling & Development, 89*(3), 318–325. https://doi.org/10.1002/j.1556-6678.2011.tb00096.x

Lopresti, A. L. (2017). Salvia (Sage): A review of its potential cognitive-enhancing and protective effects. *Drugs in R&D, 17*(1), 53–64. https://doi.org/10.1007/s40268-016-0157-5

Okun, T. (2021). White Supremacy Culture Characteristics. White Supremacy Culture. www.whitesupremacyculture.info/characteristics.html

Razack, N., & Jeffery, D. (2002). Critical race discourse and tenets for social work. *Canadian Social Work Review, 19*(2), 257–271. www.jstor.org/stable/41669763

CASE 3.3

Making Visible the Invisible
Intersectionality and Counter Storytelling of Black Girls in the Youth Justice System

KAREN M. KOLIVOSKI AND
SHERRI Y. SIMMONS-HORTON

The Situation

St. Bernadette County Department of Juvenile Justice Services (DJJS) is located in a large state with a major city, St. Bernadette City, as well as outlying suburbs and some rural farmland on the perimeter. The county population is around 200,000 people. The racial and ethnic makeup of the county is 63 percent White alone, 22 percent Black or African American alone, 18 percent Hispanic or Latino, 6 percent Asian, and 5 percent from two or more races. The median family income is comparable to the US overall at $65,000 and the percentage of persons in poverty is 20 percent. The age distribution of the population is 27 percent of people being under the age of eighteen. The youth population roughly mirrors the general population in terms of race and ethnicity and is relatively evenly split in the local Census data between boys and girls.

The DJJS is the primary agency tasked with addressing the needs of youth who become involved in the juvenile justice, or youth justice, system at every stage. The process starts when a youth enters the system, such as an arrest, and ends when they exit, such as through completing treatment or services. The mission of the agency is as follows: "To transform and improve the lives of young people while maintaining and creating safer communities and forming more equitable and just systems. This is accomplished through partnering with community-based supports, capitalizing on youths' strengths, and prioritizing youth and family assets in promotion of positive growth and development." In working to achieve this mission, DJJS is in the process of drafting a strategic plan and revisiting its data analysis and program evaluation work to assess strengths and areas of improvement.

Recently, the agency has contracted with a policy and research center that focuses on technical assistance, or targeted support on addressing a specific issue over a period of time, to youth justice agencies. The Children and Youth Justice Center (CYJC) has a national reputation for providing excellent training to youth justice leaders, offering technical assistance to local and state youth justice agencies, and conducting research and program evaluation.

At an initial meeting between DJJS and CYJC, the leadership at DJJS shared some findings by their internal data team that are of concern. Initial analysis of administrative data showed that an increasing number of girls, specifically girls of color, were receiving referrals to the youth justice system. Additional data analysis showed that these numbers increased the deeper the girls of color got into the juvenile justice system. The leaders of DJJS told CYJC staff that they are confused as delinquency is typically a "boys' issue," although they are open to gender-responsive programming. Among girls and boys, Black youth were overrepresented among the youth justice system population. A deeper dive into the administrative data showed that White youth were being referred to behavioral health services (substance abuse and mental health) at higher rates compared to Black youth. Thus, in the data, Black youth and youth who are girls seemed particularly overrepresented and are of concern to DJJS leadership.

The DJJS prides itself on being at the forefront of youth justice services and wants to address pertinent issues as they work on their strategic plan for the agency. The leaders talk about wanting to undergo a "system transformation" and having a "radical re-imagining" of the system. They told CYJC staff they "mean well" but do not see the need for a color-conscious approach in their services or treatment of youth.

Context

To better understand contemporary issues in the juvenile justice system, it is beneficial to be knowledgeable of the history and context in which it was established. The first juvenile court in the United States was formalized in Cook County, Illinois in 1899 and created a space where "a sympathetic judge could now use his discretion to apply individualized treatments to rehabilitate children, instead of punishing them" (Tanenhaus, 2002, p. 42). Reformers and advocates recognized the need for children and youth to have a separate court, as previously they would be brought under the adult criminal court, which was focused on punitive responses to law-violating behavior. Guided by the legal doctrine of *parens patriae*, Latin for "parent of the nation," the newly formed juvenile court granted the state the right to intercede in the lives of young people due to dependency (e.g., being a victim of abuse or neglect) and/or delinquency.

The main stated purpose of the juvenile court was to offer rehabilitation and protection for young people, which included informal processes and broad decision-making power from a judge who would treat each case individually and with care and concern (Center on Juvenile and Criminal Justice, 2024). The juvenile court was purposeful in establishing different terminology than the adult criminal justice system; for example, youth engage in *delinquency* instead of committing crimes, and they are not found guilty but instead are *adjudicated delinquent* (McCord et al., 2001). Despite the "admirable" goal at its founding of aspiring to provide for and protect children and youth from harm and adverse life outcomes, the juvenile justice system to this day has issues to contend with. One is the inherent conflict between social welfare, or caring for young people, and social control, or the mechanisms the system has put into place to regulate behavior in accordance with social order and norms (McCord et al., 2001). For example, Goodkind and Miller (2006) evaluated an art therapy program for incarcerated girls. The program was designed with intentions of care, particularly as some of the girls said that art was a way to express their feelings and individuality. However, there are also elements of control: due to being in confinement, the girls have limited autonomy over their daily lives, such as deciding to participate in the program, and a structured syllabus and set class agenda from the art therapist raised questions about the program's benefits.

Specifically, social control of racial and ethnic minorities has always been a focus since the founding of the juvenile court (Feld, 1999). Even before its formal founding, Houses of Refuge, early reformatories and facilities for youth, were focused on poor and delinquent young people (Center on Juvenile and Criminal Justice, 2024). Such facilities adhered to the gender and racial norms of the time and had different departments for Black youth as well as girls (Grossberg, 2002). For example, directors at the New York House of Refuge, the first juvenile reformatory in the United States, emphasized the main reason that girls came to their attention was "sexual immorality" (Grossberg, 2002, p. 17).

Involvement with the juvenile justice system has typically been composed of boys, thus programs and policies tend to be tailored around them. The 1990s saw a rise in the number of girls in juvenile justice, although system contact of both boys and girls has similarly declined in recent years (Ehrmann et al., 2019). Yet, girls account for a substantial portion of arrests in certain offenses such as larceny-theft and liquor law violations; they also comprise more than three-fourths of prostitution-related offenses (Ehrmann et al., 2019). In regard to race and ethnicity, the history of the juvenile justice system in the US is one of exclusion of young people who were not White, to a contemporary overrepresentation of youth of color.

As mentioned, the 1990s saw a rise in girls in the juvenile justice system as well as an overall increase in youth crime. This prompted a "tough on crime" response consisting of policies that included, among others, transferring youth out of the rehabilitation-focused juvenile justice system and into the more punitive-focused adult criminal justice system. Young people being incarcerated with adults places them at particular risk, and many have difficult experiences. For example, research shows that the younger a person is when confined to adult facilities, the more misbehaviors they engage in while incarcerated (Kolivoski & Shook, 2016). Since 2000, there has been a 75 percent decline in youth incarceration (Rovner, 2024). Yet, racial disparities persist, and Black girls are among the most affected (OJJDP, 2023). More recent decades of reform have focused on priorities that align with youth justice research that recognizes adolescent brain development, including treating children as children and not in adult facilities, serving children in their own homes as much as possible, and providing opportunities for youth to thrive (OJJDP Priorities, n.d.).

Intervention

Systemic interventions to address youth rehabilitation have typically reflected a punitive and carceral approach that views youth trauma-related behavior from a pathological lens. Critical Race Theory (CRT) is a lens intended to interrogate systems that specifically target racially marginalized groups. We apply specific tenets of CRT to explain the operation of anti-Black racism toward Black dual system-involved girls, and to understand the role of their lived experiences in order to better inform reimagined practice interventions. Specifically, we suggest how the tenets of *intersectionality* and *counter storytelling* can be engaged to analyze the proposed scenario between DJJS and CYJC, and how strategies can be used to apply critically informed solutions that enhance the experiences of Black system-involved girls.

Intersectionality

The concept of intersectionality is complex and has multifaceted origins and scholarly experts. In the second edition of the book *Intersectionality,* Patricia Hill Collins and Sirma Bilge define the term as "[H]ow intersecting power relations influence social relations across diverse societies as well as individual experiences in everyday life" (2020, p. 2). The roots of intersectionality's concepts include scholarship that includes Sojourner Truth's speech "Ain't I a Woman" (1851), Frances M. Beal's pamphlet "Double Jeopardy: To Be Black and Female" (1969), Toni Cade Bambara's (1970) anthology, and the Combahee River Collective (1977). The latter most notably "connected intersecting identities with interlocking systems of power" (Fischer, 2017). In a 2017 interview, Kimberlé Crenshaw, a leading CRT scholar, describes intersectionality: "Intersectionality is a lens through which you can see where power comes and collides, where it interlocks and intersects. It's not simply that there's a race problem here, a gender problem here, and a class or LBGTQ problem there. Many times, that framework erases what happens to people who are subject to all of these things" (Columbia Law School, 2017). Another definition provided by CRT scholars on intersectionality is "the examination of race, sex, class, national origin, and sexual orientation and how their combination plays out in various settings. These categories – and still others – can be separate disadvantageous factors" within a society embedded with racism, sexism, and other isms (Delgado & Stefancic, 2017, p. 58). The identities themselves are not, however, the issue. They are typically addressed as inherently negative and by which social power operates to shut out and diminish people who fall into one or more categories (Crenshaw, 1995).

Approaching an issue with an intersectional lens requires a critical perspective and acknowledging the complexities when there are multiple grounds of identity, and without it, that one is forced to choose a singular route that is not encompassing of one's true experiences where these multiple categories are critical (Crenshaw et al., 1995). Additionally, being a member of a non-dominant group that is often the target of exclusion and/or marginalization need not be a source of deficit but rather one of empowerment (Crenshaw, 1995). For instance, non-dominant group members have unique insights and experiences that offer valuable perspectives and solutions that contribute to a more just society. Last, for the purposes of this case study, we center our analysis on the intersection of race and gender, but with the acknowledgment that there are many additional intersecting identities that could and should be considered when analyzing pertinent issues.

Applying intersectionality to this case study, it is clear that although DJJS leadership seems amenable to recognizing the needs of girls in the youth justice system, they are hesitant to similarly apply a racial lens, let alone a combination of the two. A "colorblind" approach where they do not see the need to address race and ethnicity explicitly is harmful despite their well-meaning intentions. Further, an intersectional lens would require that they move beyond single silos of understanding of gender and race respectively to have a more holistic understanding of how these identities come to a confluence that exposes vulnerabilities and influences experiences and outcomes. Of note, gender and race are two of many intersecting identities to be of consideration. Echoing Nanda (2012) on girls of color in the juvenile justice system: "The starting point for this analysis is the claim that race, gender, and class intersect to create a distorted image of girls of color" (p. 1507). For example, gender stereotypes and how professionals perceive the responsibility of girls of color for their actions, agency, and openness to rehabilitation are different from how White girls are assessed (OJJDP, 2023). Girls of color, and in particular Black girls, are viewed as the problem themselves, and thus the focus of intervention, instead of being viewed as young people who have been adversely impacted by social problems (Nanda, 2012). The focus on Black girls as the problem may translate to more punitive responses and greater use of force from youth justice professionals exercising their decision-making (Epstein et al., 2017).

Counter Storytelling

The CRT tenet of counter storytelling is intended to illuminate and emphasize broad legal principles regarding race and racial/social justice. Further, counter storytelling demands that the experiential knowledge of Black and other people of color is uplifted (Reynolds & Mayweather, 2017). Counter storytelling and the use of counter narratives challenge or reject master narratives that perpetuate White privilege and underscore racist stereotypes that perpetuate the negative social construction of Black and other people of color (Goessling, 2018). One tenet of CRT posits that race is a social construct intended to bestow advantages on racially privileged groups to the detriment placed on Black groups and other groups of color on the margins of opportunity. Conversely, counter storytelling is used to interrupt and dismantle the derogatory, oppressive master narratives, and instead, heal, emancipate, and empower the racially oppressed.

Historically, the art of storytelling was a mechanism for cultures to preserve their histories and cultural sense of self through narratives that reflect the storyteller's point of view and experience (Ladson-Billings, 2021). More specifically, storytelling has consistently been a staple in marginalized communities, demonstrated in various forms. For example, Black enslaved people narrated experiences of oppression in songs and letters, and Mexican Americans wrote *corridos* or story ballads to express experiences of abuse by Texas Rangers and other White people in power (Delgado, 1989; Solorzano & Yosso, 2001). Thus, counter storytelling as a CRT tenet and method of data collection for meaningful system transformation centers on a long-held tradition of oppressed groups who understand the role of their stories as essential in their liberation. Further, the counter storytelling tenet continues in the tradition as a form of system resistance to challenge current negative discourse that perpetuates derogatory myths and stereotypes, particularly of Black individuals and communities. Increasingly, researchers committed to using scholarship to transform oppressive systems are engaging in anti-racist, qualitative, quantitative, or mixed methods designs to add to the literature on Black justice-involved girls and change the narrative that pathologized girls to one that empowers them.

As aforementioned, counter storytelling as a CRT tenet posits an urgency in moving away from harmful master narratives that perpetuate White privilege and supremacy. Counter storytelling, for example, is also a data collection method used in various qualitative designs to capture the lived experiences of oppressed individuals and communities of color. For Black justice-involved girls, personal narratives of their experiences in the juvenile system from entry to exit can provide rigorous, empirical data to record racial and gender discrimination and bias existing deeply within practices. Counter storytelling, whether within therapeutic mental health services, in programming, or research, offers Black girls a much-needed platform to use their voice to tell their stories, their way, and can inform transformative system change. Wun (2018) conducted a study through the lens of Black feminism to conduct interviews and observations with high school girls of color with school discipline records to focus on their experiences with school violence. Illuminating the lived experiences of Black system-involved girls also can underscore the strengths and empowerment of these girls despite enduring harsh and inhumane treatment in systems (Simmons-Horton et al., 2023).

Finally, mixed methods studies using anti-racist designs have allowed for a deep understanding, not only of deeply embedded oppressive practices imposed on Black girls but also offer transformative solutions that are intentional and concrete. A leading researcher with a focus on Black justice-involved girls has produced multiple mixed methods and qualitative studies that address the oppression of these girls from anti-racist frameworks including Black feminism, critical consciousness, and CRT (Goodkind, Brinkman, & Elliott, 2019; Goodkind & Miller, 2006). Research studies like these are moving the work of anti-racist informed research forward by amplifying the voices of Black girls and their unique experiences, and challenging systems and structures for broader social change.

Implications for Practice and Policy

Approaching the following case study with a CRT lens, and specifically an application of intersectionality and counter storytelling, has several implications for practice and policy related to Black girls in the youth justice system. Racism is engrained in the structures and power dynamics of US society, but every individual can play a role in a more just society. The broad concepts of systems and structures are comprised of people; people are "the system" and we each need to do our part to practice self-awareness of our own positionality as well as self-education about the role that gender, race, and its intersecting impacts have had on Black girls who come into contact with the youth justice system.

This case study has emphasized that the focus of change needs to be on systems themselves and not on the young girls and adolescents who find themselves involved in it. We need to be responsive to young people's needs, which may go beyond typical youth justice approaches of accountability and/or rehabilitation. Restorative practices, such as those that are non-adversarial and provide the youth with an opportunity to acknowledge harm and make amends in a non-punitive manner, are a start, but with emphasis on acknowledgment and action toward macro- (e.g., community, policy) level and not just micro- (e.g., individual behavior) level change. Prevention approaches could include addressing the basic needs of young people, their families, and communities, such as through universal basic income programs or affordable healthcare for everyone.

Last, applying a racial equity lens to the case study involves purposefully assessing impacts on girls of color, and particularly

Black girls in the youth justice system. The implication from such an approach is that true accountability and assessment of any progress needs to center their voices.

In applying an intersectional equity lens that centers on the unique experiences and circumstances of Black girls, publicly and privately contracted agencies and programs need to digress from traditional "cookie-cutter" strategies, and engage in culturally relevant, racially and gender-inclusive services. Researchers and communities have called for an overhaul in the training of all justice system personnel, including judges, probation officers, and attorneys. Such training should not only be trauma-informed but also include practice implementation that is reflected in decision-making processes to reduce racialized and gendered bias (Goodkind, 2019). Additional recommendations include the end to interventions which more reflect social control instead of true rehabilitation, or Black girls who are deeply engaged in the youth justice system. This includes the elimination of the shackling of girls in courtroom proceedings, providing girls with broad representation while in placements and post-disposition, and reducing probation terms (Sherman & Balck, 2015). Finally, programs are needed that promote the empowerment of Black girls that increase their consciousness of system bias against them and enhance their ability to advocate for themselves and within collectives of other Black girls with similar system experiences. One example of this form of programming is the Black Girls Equity Alliance (BGEA) in Allegheny County, in Pittsburgh, Pennsylvania. The BGEA is a collective of individuals, community-based organizations, university researchers, and government agencies that work alongside Black girls either at risk or within systems, with the goal of ending inequities that target Black girls (Goodkind, 2019). Additionally, Gwen's Girls, a non-profit organization serving Black girls in Allegheny County, responds to and serves the needs of girls through education and empowerment programming (Brinkman et al., 2019). Programming that includes after-school programs, STEM initiatives, and academic success offers gender-specific, holistic, and empowering programs that honor and center the strengths of

Black girls (Gwen's Girls, n.d.). Through working in partnership with systems of oppression to increase education and awareness of the unique experiences of Black girls, Gwen's Girls and the Black Girls Equity Alliance also involve Black girls in program development by highlighting their experiences and giving them a platform to use their stories to inform system transformation.

In summary, the overrepresentation of Black girls in the juvenile justice system is a multifaceted issue that requires a nuanced understanding of their unique situation, as well as action-oriented solutions that recognize the broader structural systems, and inherent power dynamics, in which they live. Through applying the CRT principles of intersectionality and counter storytelling, these experiences are illuminated, and disruption of harmful narratives can occur. Such an approach acknowledges the historical context and systemic biases as well as centering their voices, allowing for policies and practices that are more responsive to their needs. This also includes a shift from punitive responses to restorative practices as well as placing the focus of change on systems and the people that operate within them instead of the individual youth. Through this reframing and change in actions, the goal of a more equitable juvenile justice system that promotes opportunities so that Black girls as well as all youth can thrive is more within reach.

Discussion Questions

1. What other areas of intersectionality can you identify that factor into the issues presented in this case study (e.g., LGBTQ+, disability, biracial or multiracial considerations)?
2. What other tenets of CRT that you have learned about in this book are applicable to this case study? Are there other culturally relevant/anti-oppressive frameworks that could be applied to this case study?
3. What critiques do you have of this case study and its analysis? In other words, what does not sit right with you and why? How would you address the situation differently?
4. More broadly, what else is missing in this analysis that could be included?

REFERENCES

Beal, F. M. (Originally 1969; 2008). Double jeopardy: To be Black and female. *Meridians*, 8(2), 166–176. www.jstor.org/stable/40338758

Brinkman, B. G., Goodkind, S., Elliott, K., Joseph, A., & Doswell, W. (2019). Advocating for equity for Black girls: The formation of the Black Girls Equity Alliance. https://gwensgirls.org/wp-content/uploads/2019/10/BGEA-Report1_v4.pdf

Cade, T. [Bambara] (Ed.). (1970). *The Black woman: An anthology*. New American Library. https://archive.org/details/blackwoman00toni

Center on Juvenile and Criminal Justice. (2024). Juvenile Justice History. www.cjcj.org/history-education/juvenile-justice-history#:~:text=For%20the%20first%20half%20of,deteriorating%20conditions%2C%20and%20staff%20abuse

Collins, P. H., & Bilge, S. (2020). *Intersectionality*. John Wiley & Sons.

Columbia Law School. (2017). Kimberlé Crenshaw on Intersectionality, More Than Two Decades Later. www.law.columbia.edu/news/archive/kimberle-crenshaw-intersectionality-more-two-decades-later

The Combahee River Collective. (1977). A Black Feminist Statement (pp. 210–218).

The Combahee River Collective. (1977). A Black Feminist Statement. Capitalist Patriarchy and the Case for Socialist Feminism (pp. 362–372).

Crenshaw, K. (1989). Demarginalizing the Intersection of Race and Sex: A Black Feminist Critique of Antidiscrimination Doctrine, Feminist Theory and Antiracist Policies. University of Chicago Legal Forum, no. 1, 139–167.

Crenshaw, K. (1995). Mapping the margins. In K. Crenshaw, N. Gotanda, G. Peller, & K. Thomas (Eds.), *Critical race theory: The key writings that formed the movement*, pp. 357–383. The New Press.

Crenshaw, K., Gotanda, N., Peller, G., & Thomas, K. (Eds.). (1995). *Critical race theory: The key writings that formed the movement*. The New Press.

Delgado, R. (1989). Storytelling for oppositionists and others: A plea for narrative. *Michigan Law Review*, 87(8), 2411–2441. https://doi.org/10.2307/1289308

Delgado, R., & Stefancic, C. (2017). *Critical race theory: An introduction* (3rd ed.). New York University Press.

Ehrmann, S., Hyland, N., & Puzzanchera, C. M. (2019). Girls in the Juvenile Justice System. US Department of Justice, Office of Justice Programs, Office of Juvenile Justice and Delinquency Prevention.

Epstein, R., Blake, J., & González, T. (2017). Girlhood Interrupted: The Erasure of Black Girls' Childhood. Available at https://papers.ssrn.com/sol3/papers.cfm?abstract_id=3000695

Feld, B. C. (1999). *Bad kids: Race and the transformation of the juvenile court.* Oxford University Press.

Fischer, K. (2017). 8.2 What Is Intersectionality? LibreTexts Social Sciences. Available at https://socialsci.libretexts.org/Bookshelves/Ethnic_Studies/Introduction_to_Ethnic_Studies_(Fischer_et_al.)/08%3A_Intersectionality-_Centering_Women_of_Color/8.02%3A_What_is_Intersectionality

Goessling, K. P. (2018). Increasing the depth of field: Critical Race Theory and Photovoice as counter storytelling praxis. *The Urban Review, 50,* 648–674. https://doi.org/10.1007s11256-018-0460-2

Goodkind, S. (2019). Institutionalized Inequity: Pathways to Juvenile Justice for Black Girls in Pittsburgh and Allegheny County. Available at https://d-scholarship.pitt.edu/40910/

Goodkind, S., Brinkman, B. G., & Elliott, K. (2019). Redefining resilience and reframing resistance: Empowerment programming with Black girls to address societal inequities. *Behavioral Medicine, 46*(3-4), 317–329.

Goodkind, S., & Miller, D. L. (2006). A widening of the net of social control? "Gender-specific" treatment for young women in the US juvenile justice system. *Journal of Progressive Human Services, 17*(1), 45–70.

Grossberg, M. (2002). Changing conceptions of child welfare in the United States, 1820–1935. In >M. K. Rosenheim, F. E. Zimring, D. S. Tanenhaus, & B. Dohrn (Eds.), *A century of juvenile justice* (pp. 3–41). University of Chicago Press.

Gwen's Girls. (n.d.). https://gwensgirls.org/who-we-are/why-girls/

Hunt, S., Riegelman, A., & Myers-Kelley, S. (2024, February 28). Conducting Research through an Anti-racism Lens. University of Minnesota. https://libguides.umn.edu/antiracismlens

Kolivoski, K. M., & Shook, J. J. (2016). Incarcerating juveniles in adult prisons: Examining the relationship between age and prison behavior in transferred juveniles. *Criminal Justice and Behavior, 43*(9), 1242–1259. https://doi.org/10.1177/0093854816631793

Ladson-Billings, G. (2021). Critical race theory: What it is not!. In M. Lynn & A. D. Dixson (Eds.), *Handbook of critical racetheory in education* (2nd ed.) (pp. 32–43). Routledge. https://doi.org/10.4324/9781351032223

McCarthy, P., Schiraldi, V. N., & Shark, M. (2016). The Future of Youth Justice: A Community Based Alternative to the Youth Prison Model. www.ojp.gov/pdffiles1/nij/250142.pdf

McCord, J., Widom, C. S., & Crowell, N. A. (2001). *Juvenile crime, juvenile justice.* National Academies Press. https://doi.org/10.17226/9747

Nanda, J. (2012). Blind discretion: Girls of color & delinquency in the juvenile justice system. *UCLA Law Review, 59,* 1502–1539.

Office of Juvenile Justice and Delinquency Prevention (OJJDP). (n.d.). OJJDP Priorities. https://ojjdp.ojp.gov/about/ojjdp-priorities

Office of Juvenile Justice and Delinquency Prevention (OJJDP). (2023). Girls in the Juvenile Justice System: Literature review – A Product of the Model Programs Guide. https://ojjdp.ojp.gov/model-programs-guide/literature-reviews/girls-juvenile-justice-system

Quinn, C. R., Duron, J., Simmons-Horton, S., & Boyd, D. T. (2023). Exploring structural and systemic barriers affecting system-involved youth and families: Implications for policy and practice. In R. W. Denby-Brinsom & C. Ingram (Eds.), *Child and family serving systems: A compendium of policy and practice.* CWLA Press.

Reynolds, R., & Mayweather, D. (2017). Recounting racism, resistance, and repression: Examining the experiences and #hashtag activism of college students with critical race theory and counternarratives. *The Journal of Negro Education, 86*(3), 283–304.

Roberts, D. (2022). *Torn apart: How the child welfare system destroys Black families – And how abolition can build a safer world.* Basic Books.

Roberts, D. E. (2011). Prison, foster care, and the systemic punishment of black mothers. *UCLA Law Review, 59,* 1474.

Rovner, J. (2024). Youth Justice by the Numbers. The Sentencing Project. www.sentencingproject.org/policy-brief/youth-justice-by-the-numbers/

Sherman, F., & Balck, A. (2015). Gender Injustice: System-Level Juvenile Justice Reforms for Girls. www.defendyouthrights.org/wp-content/uploads/2015/09/Gender-Injustice-System-Level-Juvenile-Justice-Reforms-for-Girls.pdf

Simmons-Horton, S. Y., Kolivoski, K., & Garza, D. (2023). Black girl magic: Empowerment stories of black dual status girls. *Children and Youth Services Review, 152,* 107047. https://doi.org/10.1016/j.childyouth.2023.107047

Solorzano, D. G., & Yosso, T. J. (2001). Critical race and LatCrit theory and method: Counter-storytelling. *International Journal of Qualitative Studies in Education, 14*(4), 471–495.

Stewart, K. M. (2022). Re-envisioning child well-being: Dismantling the inequitable intersections among child welfare, juvenile justice, and education. *Columbia Journal of Race & Law, 12*(1). https://doi.org/10.52214/cjrl.v12i1.9925

Tanenhaus, D. S. (2002). The evolution of juvenile courts in the early twentieth century: Beyond the myth of immaculate construction. In M. K. Rosenheim, F. E. Zimring, D. S. Tanenhaus, & B. Dohrn (Eds.), *A century of juvenile justice* (pp. 42–73). University of Chicago Press.

Truth, S. (1851). Ain't I a Woman? www.nps.gov/articles/sojourner-truth.htm

Wun, C. (2018). Angered: Black and non-black girls of color at the intersection of violence and school discipline in the United States. *Race, Ethnicity, and Education, 21*(4), 423–437. https://doi.org/10.1080/13613324.2016.1248829

CASE 3.4

What Am I Missing? The Role of Intersectionality in Child Welfare Practice and Professional Relationships

KORI R. BLOOMQUIST

It was Monday morning and Kasey was preparing to start her workday – she was beginning her second week as a family reunification caseworker with Heart and Home Family Services. Heart and Home is a child welfare services agency. Broadly, child welfare refers to activities, programs, interventions, and policies intended to keep children safe and improve the well-being of children and families (Segal et al., 2019). Heart and Home provides foster care, adoption, family preservation, and family reunification services to children and families with child welfare involvement. The agency, Heart and Home, disproportionately serves women, children, and families of color. The agency's client population does not accurately reflect the population of the state but does reflect the population of those with child welfare involvement in the state, which mirrors a national reality. While White children account for half of the general child population in the United States, they make up only 44 percent of the foster care caseload and while Black or African-American children account for just 14 percent of the general child population, Black or African-American children make up nearly a quarter (23 percent) of the foster care caseload (Child Trends, 2022). Foster care is a temporary, court-monitored, out-of-home living situation for children and youth who have experienced unsafe living environments and ends when/if parents are able to provide safe, stable environments for their children (or when an alternative permanency goal is achieved) (Annie E. Casey Foundation, 2024; Child Welfare Information Gateway, n.d.-a.). Adoption is a lifelong process and refers to a formal, legal relationship between an adoptive parent(s) and child (Child Welfare Information Gateway (CWIG), 2021a; Segal et al., 2019). Family preservation services refer to activities designed to assist families in alleviating or avoiding crises to help families cope and stay together (Segal et al., 2019). If crises cannot be averted and children experience or are at risk of maltreatment, children are placed in out-of-home care.

According to the Child Abuse Prevention and Treatment Act (CAPTA), maltreatment is defined as "any recent act or failure to act on the part of a parent or caregiver that results in death, serious physical or emotional harm, sexual abuse, or exploitation, or an act or failure to act that presents an imminent risk of serious harm" (CAPTA Reauthorization Act of 2010 [P.L. 111–320] as cited in CWIG, 2022, para. 1). Child neglect is the most common type of maltreatment and is commonly defined as the failure of a parent to provide needed food, clothing, shelter, medical care, or supervision to the degree that a child's health or safety is threatened (CWIG, 2022). Family reunification, or separated families back together, is the most common goal for children in foster care (CWIG, n.d. -b.). Service provision for family reunification should be trauma-informed and use family-centered, strengths-based, culturally responsive practices (CWIG, n.d. -b.). According to the National Child Traumatic Stress Network (n.d.), a trauma-informed child welfare system is one in which all parties involved recognize and respond to the impact of trauma on those who have contact with the system, infuse and sustain trauma awareness, knowledge and skills into culture, practice, and policy, and act in collaboration and use science to maximize safety and recovery.

Kasey glanced down at her planner with the day's appointments and exhaled a heavy sigh – her fourth meeting with Shayna. Feeling a sense of dread for their impending interaction, Kasey wondered, "What Am I missing?" Kasey, a twenty-three-year-old, Caucasian woman and recent graduate of a Bachelor of Social Work (BSW) program, was excited about beginning her career as a social worker and she had a passion for working with children and families. Thus far, most of her internship and new employment experiences had been positive – she was still learning about the agency and her role and, of course, the clients with whom she was working, but things were going well – except in her work with Shayna. Shayna is twenty-eight-year-old, African American woman and mother to Caleb, a six-year-old, African American boy. Caleb was removed from the care of his mother for issues of neglect, including housing instability, food insecurity, inconsistent medical care, and being a child witness to intimate partner (domestic) violence. Reunification is the case plan, or plan for permanency, for Caleb and Shayna. In addition to the court-ordered services Shayna has already completed, including a six-week parenting course and an eight-week course for parent survivors of intimate partner violence, Shayna is ordered to participate in family reunification services including maintaining consistent communication with her service providers, obtaining stable housing, securing consistent income, and participating in bi-weekly, supervised visitations with Caleb.

Kasey strives to uphold core social work values such as service, social justice, and the importance of human relationships (NASW, 2021). While not an expert, she believes she utilizes core interpersonal qualities such as warmth, empathy, genuineness, and respect and basic interpersonal skills such as listening, attending, and observing (Chang et al., 2013) in helping relationships with clients and client systems. In most of her interactions with clients thus far, Kasey feels she has been able to build adequate rapport for collaborative work. However, with Shayna, it is different. Kasey feels as if Shayna has walls up and just does not like her – despite Kasey's initial attempts to build a relationship with kindness and a positive attitude. Kasey has completed the required assessment tools and paperwork for the first three visits – a basic biopsychosocial assessment questionnaire and a family reunification assessment tool – examining reunification risk and safety factors, visitation quality, and progress toward the permanency goal. Kasey is still new to the agency and knows these two forms are required for meetings one through three with the client, but she is not yet familiar with other tools and processes for her reunification cases and clients. Shayna has expressed frustration about having to attend three meetings in one week with Kasey. Shayna has been present and answered the tool's questions, but her answers are limited in terms of detail.

A Heart and Home colleague notices Kasey staring down at her planner and asks how she's feeling. Kasey shares that, overall, things are going well, however, and she feels guilty saying it, but she is "dreading" her meeting with Shayna today because she fears their conversation will, once again, "go nowhere" and Kasey will feel inadequate and frustrated with their lack of progress. In an attempt to cheer her up and reassure her, Kasey's colleague, Megan, quips, "it's not you, it's her – she's just difficult. Just push through. Show up to meetings with her, complete all the required paperwork, and monitor progress. If she doesn't do what she's supposed to do, that's on her. She may just make your life miserable for a while." Although Kasey appreciates the attempted support, and thanks Megan accordingly, the comments and the label, "difficult" just do not sit well with her – there has to be something else. Once again, Kasey considers, "What Am I missing in my approach with Shayna?" Kasey feels that, if she is not able to forge a connection with Shayna, their relationship, or lack thereof, will be a barrier to Caleb being reunified with his mother, an idea that leaves her feeling dejected. Kasey ponders a little longer and then stands up and walks to her supervisor's door – she knocks, and Kasey's supervisor, Dianna, looks up. Dianna has been with the agency for ten years, she is well respected by her colleagues but is new to the role of supervisor. "Would you have time to chat with me today? I am having challenges with one of my cases and I was hoping I could process it with you," Kasey shares. Dianna quickly responds, "Of course, I would be happy to meet with you, I am glad you asked. I could meet with you in an hour, would that work?" Kasey is supposed to leave for her meeting with Shayna in twenty minutes. "Actually, would you mind if I called a client quickly, I'd like to rearrange my schedule a bit to make this meeting with you work. I think meeting with you before meeting with the client again could be really beneficial," says Kasey. "Absolutely – I will hold that spot until I hear back from you," says Dianna. Kasey walks back to her desk and phones Shayna. She apologizes for the late notice, but requests that they move their meeting to tomorrow. Shayna agrees. Kasey thinks, "She's probably over the moon to avoid me today." Kasey feels some relief and also feels hopeful that, perhaps, after processing with Dianna, tomorrow's meeting with Shayna will be more productive.

Meeting with Dianna

In her meeting with Dianna, Kasey shares her concerns with Shayna's case. Kasey reveals that she feels frustrated with her interactions with Shayna and feels the work is not progressing, in large part because of their lack of a therapeutic relationship. Kasey reviews the core qualities and basic skills she attempts to employ with Shayna and all clients to build trust and rapport. Kasey also explains that she has completed the required assessment tools with Shayna, but that Shayna is very limited in her responses. Not only does Shayna seem unwilling to share with or open up to Kasey about risks, safety, visits, and motivations related to reunifying with Caleb, Shayna has not made progress with finding housing or employment. Dianna listens attentively and empathizes with Kasey's feelings of inadequacy and the fear that she will not be able to meet Shayna and Caleb's needs related to the established permanency plan of reunification. Then Dianna asks, "So, who is Shayna?" Confused and wondering if perhaps Dianna had indeed not been listening to her, Kasey responds, "Shayna. She's Caleb's mom. She's my client?" Dianna agrees and notes, "Yes, she is those things, but she is so much more, too. What do you know about her lived experiences? Which of Shayna's identities have contributed to her being Caleb's mom, being involved with the child welfare system, being your client, in a battle to be reunified with her son?" Have you investigated the role that race plays in Shayna's life, her case, or in your professional relationship?" Kasey was silent as she reflected on Dianna's questions. The answer was, she did not know. She had been so caught up with getting the required assessment forms completed in the required timeframe, and, if she was being honest, hoping Shayna would like and trust her, she failed to truly consider Shayna's past and present. And, while she did, on a somewhat unconscious level, acknowledge that Shayna was Black and she was White, she had not been intentional in thinking through or discussing race as a factor in Shayna's case or in their relationship. As a part of Kasey's privilege as a White American, she rarely has to consider her own race. "As you know, I am new to my role as supervisor", noted Dianna." "However, in my first few weeks, I have spent considerable time assessing our reunification program protocols, approaches, timelines, assessment tools, etc. and I have come to believe that, as an agency and as a program, we are not utilizing key frameworks for effective and anti-racist, anti-oppressive practices. Child welfare is rife with overrepresentations of children and families of color and those who experience poverty. To work toward socially just practices with and on behalf of our clients and communities, we must be intentional about our efforts to confront oppressive practices and to embrace an intersectionality framework in our efforts to understand and collaborate with our clients. Using an intersectionality lens can support us in acknowledging interlocking identities and experiences of oppression. I cannot guarantee that using anti-oppressive practices, including an intersectionality framework, with Shayna will improve your relationship or expedite the reunification process – however, on a micro-level of practice with Shayna, I do believe these frameworks and approaches may provide opportunities for greater understanding and collaboration. Although what you are experiencing with Shayna presents as a micro-level practice concern for you, I want you to know that I see our agency and program-based limitations regarding anti-oppressive, anti-racist, and intersectionality practice as a mezzo-level issue and I see our organization as the target of change.

I have been working with administrators and sharing ideas about our agency and its programs embracing CRT, its assumptions, and its proponents to guide our practice with clients and support us in more effective work. Our administrators have been receptive and, soon, Heart and Home will be hiring a Diversity, Equity, and Inclusion (DEI) Specialist to help us examine our policies and practices, provide training and professional development for staff, and assist us with developing and utilizing tools and measures aligned with anti-racist and anti-oppressive practices. Until we hire the specialist, and they get started on our organization's work toward transformation, administration has approved my use of some new techniques and tools with those I supervise. I'd like to share them with you and encourage you to utilize them in your work with Shayna – and all your cases. To start, let's talk about intersectionality – how familiar are you with the concept and framework of intersectionality?" asks Dianna.

Intersectionality

Proponents of CRT are committed to social justice, elevating the voices of marginalized peoples, and employing the concept of intersectionality (Delgado & Stefanic, 2001; Solórzano & Yosso, 2001, as cited in Ortiz & Jayshree, 2010). The term intersectionality was coined by law professor and civil rights activist, Kimberlé Crenshaw (1989) to describe the multiple oppressive experiences of Black women. Intersectionality has been extended to understand the overlapping and intersecting experiences of oppression for a broad range of social identities. As indicated by Crenshaw (2018), intersectionality is a metaphor for understanding the multiple forms of inequality or disadvantage that sometimes compound and create obstacles that are not understood within conventional ways of thinking. Crenshaw describes intersectionality as a prism for understanding certain kinds of problems. An intersectionality lens can be used to consider how the convergence of stereotypes about certain social identities, for example, race, class, gender, etc., may play out in social interactions and experiences. Hill-Collins (1990) advocates replacing additive (quantitative, categorizing) models of oppression with interlocking ones – which can help us think inclusively about oppressions in addition to those associated with race, class, and gender (including economic and political oppression, for example). Thus, intersectionality is not just about the intersection of multiple and diverse identities, but the oppression associated with intersecting identities. Crenshaw shares that "you can't change outcomes without understanding how they've come about" (Crenshaw, 2018, 1:50). An intersectionality framework can be used by Kasey in her work with Shayna to learn more about Shayna's multiple identities and group memberships, her lived experiences, the intersection of her oppression, and how her identities are linked to her experiences and current situation as a client in a child welfare case and a family reunification program. According to the UN Women and Partnership on the Rights of Persons with Disabilities (2022), understanding the importance of intersectionality will lead us to ask ourselves who is left behind, why, and under what circumstances.

At the Micro Level: Meeting with Shayna

In her next meeting with Shayna, Kasey approaches their interaction with a new level of interest in who Shayna is and how she arrived at their professional relationship. Kasey uses tools and questions to intentionally learn more about Shayna's life and group memberships. By purposefully attending to Shayna's experiences and multiple, varied roles, Kasey learns which social identities Shayna views as most central and most impactful in her life – including growing up in poverty, being a child witness of intimate partner violence, growing up in the foster care system, having to drop out of community college due to financial challenges, being a Black woman in the South, and being a young mother. Kasey recognizes that using an intersectionality lens for approaching her professional relationship with Shayna is not a panacea for engagement and case challenges. However, Kasey feels more connected to Shayna and their work and that she has a much better understanding of Shayna as a person and as a client. Shayna's life situation and current circumstances are not due to being only a mother or a woman or being African American. Multiple interlocking experiences of oppression have contributed to Shayna's lived experiences as well as her personhood. Kasey shares her recent successes with Shayna in a meeting with Dianna and also requests to be an active and engaged participant in future DEI initiatives at Heart and Home Family Services.

At the Mezzo Level: Agency-Based Changes

A significant body of research has documented the overrepresentation of certain racial and ethnic groups in the child welfare system (CWIG, 2021b). Researchers highlight a legacy of interconnected oppressions faced by women, children, and families of color and highlight the role that race, gender, and class have played in passing key child welfare policies (including Social Security Act Title IV and V, 1935; The Flemming Rule, 1960; CAPTA, 1974; Indian Child Welfare Act (ICWA), 1978; Multiethnic Placement Act (MEPA), 1994; Interethnic Placement Act (IPA), 1996, and Adoption and Safe Families Act (ASFA), 1997) and in the overrepresentation of poor Black women, children, and families in the child welfare system (Williams-Butler et al., 2024). CRT asks us to examine how and why practices and policies were created – and whom they ultimately serve – as a means of challenging institutionalized forms of oppression (Portland Community College, n.d.).

To support transformation and sustainable change in the areas of diversity, equity, and inclusion, including learning, embracing, and employing anti-racist and anti-oppressive practices at the agency level, Heart and Home hired a Diversity, Equity, and Inclusion Specialist. Under the leadership of the Specialist, Heart and Home Family Services completed a comprehensive agency cultural and climate assessment. Results of the assessment informed strategies for change. Professional development, tuition assistance, and leadership programs were developed and implemented to elevate the knowledge, skill, and positions of employees of color within the agency. An equity committee was developed and implemented to support critical consciousness among agency executives and to develop group goals for systemic change. The agency also revised DEI training to meet employees where they were in terms of DEI knowledge and skill, creating multiple learning and growth pathways (introductory, intermediate, and advanced). All DEI pathways include content regarding intersectionality and power and privilege. Completion of a DEI pathway became a criterion for employment with Heart and Home and is reviewed annually in employees' performance evaluations. Lastly, in line with critical practice principles for anti-oppressive practices (Matthews et al., 2020), including assessing clients' experiences of oppression, empowering services users, and working in partnership, Heart and Home recruited current and former clients to serve on a lived-experience collaborator committee – elevating the voices of those with lived child welfare experience and considering the unique perspectives of those impacted by child welfare policies and practices. In an effort to support social justice, Heart and Home Family Services made a commitment to creating change at both the individual and system levels of practice. Dianna recognizes that the agency has a long way to go toward true transformational change, but feels, in alignment with elements of anti-oppressive practice, Heart and Home is working toward institutional change as a means to achieving broader social change (Matthews et al., 2020).

Implications for Practice

Disproportionality and disparity for children and youth of color are significant concerns in child welfare. In particular, American Indian, Alaska Native, and African American children are over-represented in the child welfare system and experience disparate treatment when involved (CWIG, 2021b). Racial disparities occur at nearly every significant decision-making point across the continuum of child welfare practice (CWIG, 2021c). Black children in the United States experience higher rates of child welfare investigation, removal from their families of origin, termination of parental rights, placement moves, fewer appropriate services, and are less likely to be reunified with their parents compared to White children (White & Persson, 2022). Given that African American children are less likely to exit foster care through reunification than White children, increasing reunification rates for African American families is one way to address racial disproportionality and disparity in child welfare cases (CWIG, n.d. -b). American Indian and Alaska Native children are also overrepresented in foster care, making up 2 percent of those in care and 1 percent of the child population in the United States (Annie E. Casey Foundation, 2023). According to the Child Welfare Information Gateway (2021c), a variety of factors likely contribute to issues of racial and ethnic disproportionality and disparity – including that child welfare has not historically used an anti-racist approach to practice or utilized perspectives of those with lived experience. To confront pervasive and persistent issues of disproportionality and disparity for children and families of color in child welfare, an intersectionality framework for examining how, at a minimum, race, gender, and class contribute to inequities is required. Racialized, gendered, and class-based policies and biases in case-based decision-making perpetuate overrepresentation and poor outcomes for children and families. To promote social justice and systemic transformations in child welfare, CRT, including an intersectionality framework and anti-oppressive practices, must be at the forefront of policy analysis and the development and implementation of training and education for child welfare leaders and professionals. A failure to employ intersectional and anti-oppressive approaches will result in the perpetuation of disparities in child welfare and ultimately in the undermining of the child, youth, family, and community well-being.

Discussion Questions

1. How might using an intersectionality framework for approaching work with clients and client systems aid engagement and relationship building?
2. What are some of the overlapping and intersecting identities of vulnerability for the population of children and youth with child welfare involvement?
3. What forms of inequality do you believe may influence child welfare system involvement?
4. How can agency policies and practices hinder anti-oppressive practice? How can agency policies and practices advance anti-oppressive practice?
5. How can mezzo-level, agency-based change affect practice at the micro level with clients? How can mezzo-level, agency-based change affect practice at the macro level with systems?

REFERENCES

Annie E. Casey Foundation. (2023). A Look at the Latest Population Trends for Native Children. www.aecf.org/blog/a-look-at-the-latest-population-trends-for-native-children#:~:text=Over%20the%20last%20two%20decades,has%20remained%20steady%20at%201%25

Annie E. Casey Foundation. (2024). Foster Care Explained: What Is It, How It Works and How It Can Be Improved. www.aecf.org/blog/what-is-foster-care

Chang, V. N., Scott, S. T., & Decker, C. L. (2013). *Developing helping skills: A step by step approach* (2nd ed.). Brooks/Cole.

Child Trends. (2022). State-Level Data for Understanding Child Welfare in the United States. Companion Guide. Chromeextension://efaidnbmnnnibpcajpcglclefindmkaj/https://cms.childtrends.org/wp-content/uploads/2022/02/ChildWelfareDataCompanionGuide_ChildTrends_March2022.pdf

Child Welfare Information Gateway. (2021a). Adoption. www.childwelfare.gov/topics/permanency/adoption/

Child Welfare Information Gateway. (2021b). Addressing Disproportionality. www.childwelfare.gov/topics/equitable-practice/addressing-disproportionality/

Child Welfare Information Gateway. (2021c). Child Welfare Practice to Address Racial Disproportionality and Disparity. www.childwelfare.gov/resources/child-welfare-practice-address-racial-disproportionality-and-disparity/

Child Welfare Information Gateway. (2022). Definitions of Child Abuse and Neglect. US Department of Health and Human Services, Administration for Children and Families, Children's Bureau. www.childwelfare.gov/topics/systemwide/laws-policies/statutes/define/

Child Welfare Information Gateway. n.d. -a. Foster Care. www.childwelfare.gov/topics/permanency/foster-care/

Child Welfare Information Gateway. n.d. -b. Reunifying Families. www.childwelfare.gov/topics/permanency/reunifying-families/

Crenshaw, K. (1989). Demarginalizing the intersection of race and sex: A black feminist critique of antidiscrimination doctrine, feminist theory and antiracist politics. *University of Chicago Legal Forum, 1*(8).

Crenshaw, K. (2018, June, 22). Kimberlé Crenshaw: What Is Intersectionality? [Video]. YouTube. www.youtube.com/watch?v=ViDtnfQ9FHc

Delgado, R. & Stefancic, J. (2001). *Critical race theory: An introduction.* NYU Press.

Hill-Collins, P. (1990). *Black feminist thought: Knowledge, consciousness, and the politics of empowerment* (1st ed.). Routledge.

Matthews, H., Sibbald, S., Szoke, T., & Varela, S. T. (2020). Anti-oppressive Practice. Critically Infused Social Work. www.criticallyinfusedsw.com/antioppressive-practice

National Association of Social Workers. (2021). *Code of ethics.* NASW Press. www.socialworkers.org/About/Ethics/Code-of-Ethics/Code-of-Ethics English

National Child Traumatic Stress Network. (n.d.). Creating Trauma-Informed Systems. www.nctsn.org/trauma-informed-care/creating-trauma-informed-systems

Ortiz, L., & Jayshree, J. (2010). Critical race theory: A transformational model for teaching diversity. *Journal of Social Work Education, 46*(2), 175–193.

Portland Community College. (n.d.). Take 5: Critical Race Theory (CRT) Decision- Making Toolkit. People Strategy, Equity, and Culture. www.pcc.edu/hr/culture-transformation-development/take-5-critical-race-theory-toolkit/

Segal, E. A., Gerdes, K. E., & Steiner, S. (2019). *An introduction to the profession of social work: Becoming a change agent* (6th ed.). Cengage: Boston.

Solorzano, D. G., & Yosso, T. J. (2001). Critical race and LatCrit theory and method: Counter-storytelling – Chicana and Chicano graduate school experiences. *International Journal of Qualitative Studies in Education*, 14(4), 471–495. https://doi.org/10.1080/09518390110063365

UN Women & Partnership on the Rights of Persons with Disabilities. (2022). Intersectionality Resource Guide and Toolkit. www.unwomen.org/sites/default/files/2022-01/Intersectionality-resource-guide-and-toolkit-en.pdf

White, S., & Persson, S. M. (2022). *Racial discrimination in child welfare is a human rights violation: Let's talk about it that way.* American Bar Association. www.americanbar.org/groups/litigation/resources/newsletters/childrens-rights/racial-discrimination-child-welfare-human-rights-violation-lets-talk-about-it-way/

Williams-Butler, A., Golden, K. E., Mendez, A., & Stevens, B. (2024). Intersectionality and child welfare policy: Implications for black women, children, and families. *Child Welfare*, 98(4), 75–96.

CASE 3.5

Don't Forget to Shine!
The Intersection of Race, Age, and Sexuality at the End of Life

SARA J. ENGLISH

> *Any human act that gives rise to something new is referred to as a creative act.*
>
> *Lev Vygotsky*

Race as a Social Construct

Social constructivism explores how knowledge and understanding is created through collaborative agreement (Vygotsky, 1962). Social constructivism sees concepts, ideas, and beliefs as things that are created and maintained within a social environment. What is true is what is perceived to be true, and what is perceived to be true varies from place to place. In short, truth is subjective, and subjective truth is dynamic. This meaning-making is an active process, which builds through interactions. This understanding can be applied to explain how people make meaning about race, the understanding of race, and the perception of race. According to CRT, this social construction of race has a powerful impact on people's lived experiences (Haney-Lopez, 2000).

Meaning and understanding changes as socially agreed-upon definitions change and evolve, with the agreed-upon definitions influencing the attitudes, perceptions, and expectations we have for ourselves and others. The social environment frames our beliefs, and our beliefs are built through our interactions with others – and the experiences – we have within that social environment, and these interactions and experiences reinforce what we perceive to be true. How individuals and communities view race is created and maintained within a social environment, with the environment influencing perceptions of individuals and individuals influencing the environment. This linked understanding builds a continuous loop of belief – a *construction* – which is supported through social learning, where understanding develops from a process of observation, imitation, and repetition (Bandura, 1977; Vygotsky, 1962).

Social constructivism sees truth as something that is created through social agreements. Many theorists discuss social constructivism and how socially influenced definitions of truths can build both barriers and bridges to understanding (Guess, 2006; Levy et al., 2017). While bridges can create new ways of being and understanding, barriers can support entrenched bias and discrimination for persons, especially among Black persons who are often socially sifted through observable characteristics. Guess (2006) explored race-based social hierarchies, noting that social constructs become fixed by dominant groups, with bias and racism passing over time, leading to generational racialized experiences and perceptions, and that "among most descendants of the formerly enslaved, there continues to exist a social hierarchy based on skin color … the myth of light-complected people implying something better than, or above, dark-complected people" (p. 671).

Race is often perceived, based upon what is observed. What someone looks like, sounds like, acts like, or appears to be, leads to shortcuts of understanding. Race – or the perception of race – is based upon observable characteristics that are attributed to behaviors. As Bakker (2020) explained, perceptions of race are social constructions and invented understandings that are based upon social agreements, with the idea of race

> deemed to be located in phenotypical difference (which includes such markers as skin color and hair texture), there is no biological basis for race or for the differentiation of groups of people along racial lines. Rather, the decisions to characterize and mark a group of people as 'black,' others as 'brown,' and yet others as 'white' are grounded in a set of sociopolitical processes. (p. 482)

Black individuals have endured bad or negative social construction for centuries. For example, they have been viewed as bad, dishonest, criminals, and loose. On the contrary, being White has been associated with good, honest, and the moral standard for other races (Yancy & Butler, 2015). According to CRT, the negative construction of Black individuals, relative to their White counterparts, impact how persons are treated by others within a social environment, and the perceptions people have of them. This is further compounded for Black people who have a *clustering* of social disadvantages, or an intersection of oppressed identities (Wolff & deShallit, 2007).

This case explores the concept of family through multiple intersections, including race, sexual identity, and religion, asking students to examine the meaning of family and how that concept is created and maintained through social constructions of race, how the concept may change (or needs to change), and how social expectations of family are dynamic, with rules that create both barriers and bridges for persons living within a social environment. What is family? How do we build it? How do we recognize families who may look different? Specifically, how is the idea of *family* constructed for Black people, how is that addressed for LGBTQ+ couples, and in what ways does it influence decisions of care?

The Case

The Problem

Bonita Smith was a newly graduated MSW, working on her license. She was also new to medical social work, having worked at the hospital for only a few weeks. So far, she loved her job, where she helped persons figure out the "next steps" after they had been admitted to the hospital for a serious concern. She was one of six discharge social workers at the hospital. Patients usually transferred to her care when they became stable enough to move out of intensive care or emergency services. Although she was still learning, Bonita was happy that one of her colleagues, Liz Brown, was also her licensing supervisor. In the short time that she had been at the hospital, Liz had become a trusted mentor. Bonita wanted to do everything well and she made sure she carefully evaluated the needs of the patients with whom she worked. She took her job seriously. She wanted to get it right.

Most of the persons under Bonita's caseload were older and were recovering from falls or some kind of traumatic injury. Some had signs of dementia. Almost all needed more care than they could receive in their own home.

Over the short time she had worked at the hospital, Bonita had discovered that the healthcare system seemed to count on family members to fill in as caregivers. This was a problem. Not everyone had family who could – or would – fill this need, and many folks did not get the care they deserved.

As Bonita scanned the patient transfer information, she saw that this was certainly true for her new patient, who was recovering from a recent ischemic stroke, which affected her speech and movement. The discharge nurse informed Bonita that the patient had recently transferred from the intensive care unit (ICU) and into a standard hospital room, on the wing where Bonita worked. Liz Brown was the medical social worker for the ICU, and she filled Bonita in on the patient's progress. "She seems to have good days and bad days," said Liz. "Give me a call if you need any help with this one." Liz started down the hall, then turned. "Oh, I finally got hold of her brother. He's her only family member and he's supposed to be here tomorrow. John Troutman. He's coming from Texas."

As Bonita looked over the electronic records, she couldn't believe her eyes. Toni Trulove. Toni Trulove? Toni Trulove! Toni was a star – at least she was to Bonita, who had spent every Friday night of her teen years watching Toni on Channel 10, hosting *Lights, Camera, Fashion with Toni Trulove*. *Lights, Camera, Fashion* was a local version of *Elvira: Mistress of the Dark*, only with more sequins. When Bonita was growing up, she and her friends would gather around the television on Friday nights, huddling together as Toni introduced them to Bette Davis, Dorothy Dandridge, Kathryn Hepburn, Barbara Stanwyck, Mae West and the beauty of old Hollywood. Toni talked about the movies, shared stories about the stars, and demonstrated the magic of hair and makeup. Each week ended with Toni's reminder to the audience "I am glam and so are YOU! Until we meet again, don't forget to shine!" *Don't forget to shine*, Bonita smiled, as she walked toward the unit where Ms. Toni Trulove had been transferred. On her way, she stopped to speak with Betty, the nurse aid who was on duty.

"She can't really do much for herself," said Betty. "I had to help her with everything – bathing, dressing, all of it. Her whole left side is pretty much gone." It was clear that Ms. Trulove was not ready to go home, at least not without significant care. Her medical insurance would pay for services at a rehabilitation center for up to ninety days, which would at least provide some time to figure out if she would be able to return to her home. *If* she returned home. Ms. Trulove was stable enough to move out of ICU, but she had experienced some significant damage from this stroke. Home was a long way off.

Toni Trulove was a seventy-two-year-old, unmarried, Black transgender woman, who had no children. Although her medical records noted her as healthy, this was Ms. Trulove's second hospitalization in four years, and her second stroke within the past eight months. The MRI results from this most recent event had not made it into the electronic record yet, and the extent of damage wasn't clear, but the current nurses' notes echoed Betty's concern about Ms. Trulove's need for assistance to bathe, dress, groom, eat, toilet, and transfer. Liz's notes from the ICU mentioned some problems with cognition that were not easily explained. At times, the patient's affect was flat and she often failed to respond to direct questions. At other times, she would speak slowly but was able to get her message out. Most of the time, it appeared that Ms. Trulove followed what was going on, but that was inconsistent, too. Right now, Bonita was on the way to meet with her to discuss a potential discharge to a local rehabilitation center at Sunflower Manor, a large local nursing home. Bonita estimated that Toni Trulove would be scheduled for discharge in about three days and if she could not fully understand the discharge plan, her next of kin would need to step up.

Toni Trulove! Bonita smiled as she walked down the hall. Bonita was on her way to meet Toni Trulove and Pearl Estes, Ms. Trulove's life partner and more recently, Ms. Trulove's primary caregiver. Both women were worried. Although there was insurance, there was no will, no power of attorney, and no durable power of attorney for healthcare. Toni Trulove needed help.

As Bonita entered the room, she could see that Ms. Toni Trulove was ready for whatever the day would bring. She was dressed in a silk robe, with full makeup, and jewelry. Despite the clear damage to the left side of her face, she was glam and she was shining. She welcomed Bonita and beckoned her to sit close, so she could hear. "My left side is a little weak," Toni explained. Bonita checked her iPad and began to ask the standard discharge questions – What were her plans? Who did she have to help? How well did she think she could make it at home? After a few questions, Toni raised her hand. "Let's dispense with all that, at least for now, mmm? There is a more pressing problem. We need some help." Toni nodded to Pearl, and Pearl began.

Toni Trulove and Pearl Estes had been together since they met in Malibu. "We have a grand story," Pearl smiled as she shared, "I was walking up from the beach and came across this rough looking person in the parking lot." Toni nodded and looked straight ahead.

"Rough and dirty, windblown and all that. A real mess but an instant connection," laughed Pearl, her large brown eyes sparking. She touched Toni's arm gently and asked, "You left Texas right after graduation, isn't that right?"

Toni was engaged now, replying, "Oh, I hopped on that old motorcycle and didn't stop until I saw the sea." "The ocean," Pearl corrected. "Yes, the ocean," said Toni. "I was Tony then," Toni said, as she reached for Pearl's hand. "I had to leave that place, those people. I had to find my own way, and on the way, I found you, my beautiful Black pearl. It has been forever, hasn't it?"

During their time together, Bonita learned about their life together and she listened to their concerns about whether the nursing home staff would care for her kindly, whether going to the Sunflower Manor was a good idea. Toni sometimes struggled to speak, and Bonita wasn't always sure if Toni was following what was going on. She slurred many of her words, and Pearl began to speak for her: "We wanted to speak to you because we know that some decisions need to be made. Toni's brother, John, is her next of kin. Legally, anyway. But she hasn't spoken to him in years. He didn't like Toni. He didn't like her friends. He didn't like me. He didn't like what he called 'our lifestyle.' It was a lot harder to be out back then, especially as a Black person. Anyway, after Tony decided to live as Toni, well ... her old family didn't approve, so that was the end of that. Told us Toni wasn't family anymore. Said I wasn't welcome, either. We aren't fitting to them. We don't even fit in the church." Pearl fell quiet, shook her head, and continued. "And they totally cut us off when she started the show ... long story short, we made our own family, and Toni is the head of the pack. Look, Toni doesn't want John to strut on in and make the decisions." Pearl looked at Toni, who was blankly staring into space. "I can't believe he has the nerve to come here, I really can't."

Pearl began to whisper, adding: "If something were to happen ... if Toni had another stroke or something else, I wouldn't be able to help make decisions. You know, John is worse than the rest of them. He's never even met me. I only talked to him once on the phone. Let me tell you, once was enough! He cussed me out and said it was my fault that Toni was such a sinner. He swore he never would meet any of her friends." Pearl stopped again. "I guess we thought we would live forever. We probably should have gotten married, you know, signed some forms, but we just never did. I don't know why we never did. Toni and I don't have a will or anything, and I just don't know what will happen if she has another stroke or gets to the point where she can't make any decisions."

"I am dying," Toni said slowly, still looking at the wall. "There's not an unfathomable amount, but there's enough. There's the house and the property. And the things in the warehouse. There are people I want to take care of, and I have been terribly negligent. My family – my real family – are the people who know me and who love me as I am. I am, frankly, afraid that I will end up back in that dusty town, with a dusty old dead name carved into some tombstone, you know?"

Toni turned and smiled at Pearl. Pearl looked like she was holding back tears, but she smiled back. Then, Toni turned toward the wall again, staring blankly at the nothingness. "I just love her so much," Pearl said softly, as she began to weep. "We are a family! We are our own family. We deserve to be treated that way. Toni's my family; she's my best friend. My only friend, really. In my heart, I'm her wife. We just want to be able to make some decisions before it's too late. And we need some help."

A few minutes later, Bonita walked down the hallway. The empty elevator allowed her a few moments of silence, and she considered Toni and Pearl and the things left undone. Bonita wasn't sure if she could be of much help, but she was going to try. As she walked, Bonita considered the way family could take the shine out of life, and how she did not want Ms. Toni Trulove's last days to be without any shine.

Beginning to Tackle the Problem

Bonita knew she had to move fast. John was on his way, and it looked like Toni was getting worse by the minute. Bonita made her way to

Liz's office as quickly as she could. While Bonita waited, she began to search for information. She looked up information on family estrangement and learned that about half of all LGBTQ+ adults are estranged from their family of origin. Transgender persons experience even greater estrangement (Chapman, 2021; Fasullo, 2021). Peterson and Holloway (2021) found that older LGBTQ+ persons frequently experience estrangement both from their biological family and from their religious home, resulting in trauma and distrust of institutions. This distrust can be a barrier for persons to seek legal support that may offer protection.

Though these experiences may extend across the LGBTQ+ population, they may be more keenly experienced for older LGBTQ+ persons who are transgender and Black. "Every single thing Toni and Pearl have experienced, just seems to make this harder," thought Bonita. As a social worker, Bonita knew that problems – especially *wicked problems* that are entrenched and complex – need to be addressed on multiple levels of engagement. She started to outline some strategies for assisting Toni and Pearl and waited to check in with Liz about ways to meet their immediate and emerging needs.

Implications for Practice

The concept of family is a social construct, created and maintained by social norms that inform our individual attitudes, perceptions, and expectations of what a family *is* or *is not*. Although there is a strong history of advocacy in the Black queer community, families who identify as more traditional may struggle with acceptance of LGBTQ+ persons. Quinn and colleagues (2016) noted how traditional Black cultures promote social constructs of what the social and sexual roles of a man or a woman are. Additionally, the influence of the Black Church strongly emphasizes and reinforces these social constructs (Quinn et al., 2016). In most cultures, family is considered persons who are related by blood or marriage. The United States Health Resources and Services Administration (2023) stated that

"A family is a group of two or more persons related by birth, marriage, or adoption who live together," with persons not meeting this definition being "unrelated individuals" (paras. 1–3). This narrow definition is shared by many government institutions and various organizations and reflects entrenched social expectations. Determinations of family often inform plans of care and legal expectations. Yet not every person has a positive relationship with relations of birth, marriage, or adoption.

A recent survey of members of the LGBTQ+ community found that almost half reported estrangement with at least one family member, with half of respondents reporting having no close relationships with family (Just Like Us, 2023). Chapman (2021) found that the impact of estrangement on Black members of the LGBTQ+ community is difficult to know, due to distrust and a reluctance to report estrangement. These reports echo research demonstrating high rates of ambivalent, estranged, or strained relationships between LGBTQ+ persons and family members (Bosley-Smith & Reczek, 2022; Boza & Nicholson Perry, 2014), with transgender persons experiencing even higher rates of frail, fragmented, or fractured relationships with kin (Masa et al., 2023). Family estrangement is associated with higher rates of depression, anxiety, loneliness, isolation, and suicidal behavior. Masa and colleagues (2023) also reported that these risks can be persistent across the lifespan, particularly among Black individuals who due to the way they are negatively socially constructed, face implicit and explicit bias and discrimination across the lifespan. Yet, this risk can be offset through the establishment of mutual, trusting relationships with others – a chosen family. One's chosen family can include friends, lovers, life partners, or others who provide social support that influence "the infrastructure of one's physical and psychosocial well-being" (English, 2023, pp. 126), providing supportive care to promote emotional and physical health.

Being aware of the role of negative social construction on Black individuals' ability to thrive in society and considering and honoring the roles of persons who are part of one's chosen family is essential for practice. This is especially true in spaces where chosen family are given little to no legal consideration. Social workers can advocate for the formal inclusion of chosen family, helping persons face challenges, linking them to services, and assisting persons in obtaining legal documentation that allows one's chosen family members to be legally recognized, especially in situations involving decisions of care.

Discussion Questions

1. How can you consider race as a social construction when seeking to address the needs of Toni Trulove?
2. What is Bonita's ethical obligation to Toni? Why?
3. What information could Bonita share with Toni and Pearl that might help them make decisions regarding Toni's health?
4. What steps can the social worker take to help clients cope with negative social constructions of race, particularly with Black families?
5. What other systems in society can the social construction of race impact?

REFERENCES

Bakker, J. M. (2020). Hidden presence: Race and/in the history, construct, and study of western esotericism. *Religion, 50*(4), 479–503.

Bandura, A. (1977). *Social learning theory*. Prentiss-Hall.

Bosley-Smith, E., & Reczek, R. (2022). Why LGBTQ adults keep ambivalent ties with parents: Theorizing "Solidarity Rationales". *Social Problems, 2022*, spac007. https://doi.org/10.1111/jomf.12898

Boza, C., & Nicholson Perry, K. (2014). Gender-related victimization, perceived social support, and predictors of depression among transgender Australians. *International Journal of Transgenderism, 15*, 25–52.

Chapman, F. S. (2021). *Brothers, sisters, strangers: Sibling estrangement and the road to reconciliation*. Viking.

English, S. J. (2023). Kithship: Protective aspects of a family of choice for older transgender persons. In M. P. Moreau, C. Lee, & C. Okpokiri (Eds.), *Reinventing the family in uncertain times*. Bloomsbury.

Fasullo, K. (2021, September). *Q & A with Katie Fusullo: Needs of older LGBTQ older adults and long-term care*. SAGE. www.sageusa.org/what-we-do/national-resource-center-on-lgbt-aging/

Guess, T. J. (2006). The social construction of whiteness: Racism by intent, racism by consequence. *Critical Sociology, 32*(4), 649–673. https://diversity.umsl.edu/documents/W07_Guess_article_s6.pdf

Just Like Us (2023). New Research Shows Almost Half LGBT+ Adults Are Estranged from Family and a Third "Not Confident" Their Parents Will Accept Them. www.justlikeus.org/blog/2023/04/19/new-research-shows-almost-half-of-lgbt-adults-are-estranged-from-family-and-a-third-not-confident-their-parents-will-accept-them/

Levy, A., Saguy, T., Halperin, E., & van Zomeren, M. (2017). Bridges or barriers? Conceptualization of the role of multiple identity gateway groups in intergroup relations. *Frontiers in Psychology, 8*, 1097. www.frontiersin.org/journals/psychology/articles/10.3389/fpsyg.2017.01097/full

Haney-Lopez, I. (2000). The social construction of race. In R. Delgado & J. Stefancic (Eds.), *Critical race theory: The Cutting Edge* (2nd ed.) (pp. 163–175). Temple University Press.

Masa, R., Baca-Atlas, S. N., Shangani, S., Forte, A. B., & Operario, D. (2023). Family rejection, socioeconomic precarity, and exchanging sex for food among young transgender adults: Findings from the U.S. Transgender Survey. *Journal of Health Care for the Poor and Underserved, 34*(2), 549–568.

Peterson, S., & Holloway, I. W. (2021). Social work practice with sexual minority men. In S. J. Dodd (Ed.), *The Routledge international handbook of social work and sexualities* (pp. 84–96). Routledge.

Quinn, K., Dickson-Gomez, J., & Kelley, J. A. (2016). The role of the Black church in the lives of young Black men who have sex with men. *Culture, Health & Sexuality, 18*(5), 524–237. https://pubmed.ncbi.nlm.nih.gov/26489851/

United States Health Resources and Services Administration. (2023). Definition of Family. www.hrsa.gov/get-health-care/affordable/hill-burton/family

Vygotsky, L. S. (1962). *Thought and language* (Hanfmann, E. & Vakar, G., Trans.). MIT Press.

Vygotsky, L. (1978). *Mind in society*. Harvard University Press.

Wolff, J., & deShalit, A. (2007). *Disadvantage*. Oxford University Press.

Yancy, G., & Butler, J. (2015, January 12). What's Wrong with "All Lives Matter?" The Stone. http://opinionator.blogs.nytimes.com/2015/01/12/whats-wrong-with-all-livesmatter/#more-155504

PART IV

Case Studies in
Macro-Level Practice

CASE 4.1

What's in It for Us? A Case of Interest Convergence

MONIQUE A. CONSTANCE-HUGGINS

Interest Convergence

The tenet of interest convergence suggests that dominant culture only supports civil rights advances for minoritized groups when they simultaneously stand to benefit from those advances. Conversely, minoritized groups do not receive support for policies and programs that advance them if there are no benefits in those advances for the dominant group (Bell, 1980; Delgado & Stefancic, 2017). Civil rights advances such as Brown vs. Board of Education provide an example of converging interest. Specifically, mainstream America supported this move to desegregate school, which advanced Black interest, because it simultaneously improved the world image of the US during the Cold War period. The concept of interest convergence can also be applied to Americans doing international work. In such cases, policies and programs that support international communities also serve to advance the interest of Americans.

A Beautiful Island

St. Vincent and the Grenadines is a beautiful, small island that is located in the Eastern Caribbean. It is comprised of a larger island, St. Vincent, and a chain of thirty-two smaller islands, called the Grenadines. The country is about 138 square miles and has a population of about 110,000 people. Tourism and agriculture provide the economic backbone for this developing country. Having such an economic landscape, however, means that St. Vincent and the Grenadines is economically fragile due to increasing natural disasters. Not only does the country have to contend with frequent hurricanes, but also there is the threat of the active volcano – La Soufrière. When a hurricane strikes, it damages properties, infrastructure and the beaches as well as destroying crops. When the volcano erupts, ash covers the beaches, causes house roofs to sink in, and overwhelms the crops and livestock. The latter was the case in April 2021, when La Soufrière had an explosive eruption.

The volcano affected many of the northern communities of the island. These communities are north of the Rabacca Dry River, which means they are often cut off from adequate resources that the rest of the island may enjoy. The northern region is also the home of most of the descendants of the Kalinago and Garifuna, the Indigenous people of St. Vincent and the Grenadines. As volcanic ash rained down on these villages, residents quickly packed up some of their belongings and hustled to waiting buses that would carry them to the nearest safe areas. They left behind villages covered in ashes. The once lush green hillside that was dotted with banana and coconut trees as well as root crops now had a thick blanket of ashes. Not only were the crops affected, so were the animals. House roofs started to cave in under the heavy weight of the ashes. Further, schools, churches, and shops were closed.

St. Vincent's northern communities had seen their fair share of setbacks. In 1979, the previous time when La Soufrière erupted, these areas had also buckled under the weight of volcanic eruption. Similar to 2021, buildings were destroyed, and people's livelihoods were disrupted. People who had lost everything had to relocate to areas in the southern part of the island, closer to the capital city of Kingstown. Given that these northern communities are among the poorest in St. Vincent, they had a very long and daunting road to recovery. Even the churches and local organizations in the communities, which often provided emotional and tangible assistance to residents, found themselves too overwhelmed to assist.

Help Still Needed

More than a year after La Soufrière had its explosive eruption in 2021, life had not returned to "normal" for many residents north of the Rabacca Dry River. In fact, some families had still not fully returned to the villages. Many buildings were still in disrepair, and farmers had not been able to amass a decent level of livestock to improve their livelihood. The government struggled to provide adequate assistance as the COVID-19 pandemic also put a strain on the already fragile economy. The eruption of La Soufrière had exacerbated these economic struggles, which increased the country's economic and social vulnerability and created more need for foreign assistance. Assistance came from many Vincentians living abroad as well as from American non-profit organizations. One such organization was Olive Branch.

What's in It for Us?

Olive Branch was a relatively young organization. It existed primarily to provide disaster relief assistance to communities in the US. The organization saw this as a need given the increasing number of devastating natural disasters within the last couple of years. Its efforts, however, were not just local; the organization was also open to the possibility of working internationally. The organization felt that working internationally would help to increase its influence and impact. After hearing about the eruption of La Soufrière on several news outlets, and being motivated by some of its own interests, the organization decided to send a small team of disaster workers to work primarily in the northern areas of St. Vincent and the Grenadines. The Director, Bill Drew, thought it would be a good opportunity to make inroads into the world of disaster recovery. After all, the country of St. Vincent and the Grenadines is relatively close to the US, there is no language barrier, and the government and people are open to foreign assistance. "This should be an easy entry," he said to himself. He then started inquiring about contacts in St. Vincent and the Grenadines. That is when he was connected with Ms. Smith, the president of the Northern Communities Progressive Organization (NCPO).

The NCPO

This organization had been in existence for about fifteen years. Its main purpose was to provide empowerment programs to youths in the northern communities. It provided job training, skills development, and education classes to youths with the hopes of equipping them for the job market. In addition to targeting the youth, the organization had an equally important aim of providing emotional and tangible support for members of the blind community. Some of the specific things it did for this community were to teach them skills such as basket weaving and jewelry making. It even provided light meals once a week to a limited number of people in the community who were in need. Through generous donations from Vincentians living at home and abroad, the organization was able to build a community center, through which it was able to offer its services. Beyond serving as a hub to provide services, the community center offered a gathering place for young people and members of the blind community to find support from each other. If people were not inside participating in an activity, they were outside sitting on the large rock under the mango tree, just "liming" (the Caribbean word for hanging out). Now, the eruption of La Soufrière had not only destroyed the homes for many people of the northern communities, but it also destroyed their home away from home – the NCPO. Building back the center was key for Ms. Smith, the president, and the rest of the community, but working with disaster workers was not going according to plan.

Boots on the Ground

A team of four White men from Olive Branch arrived in St. Vincent and the Grenadines excited about the opportunity to do work. They met with Ms. Smith who talked about the northern communities, the NCPO, and their greatest needs in the rebuilding process. The team then spent the next couple of days walking through the communities and doing their own assessment of what they thought needed to be done. Their first point of business was to work on the community center. As the work went on, Ms. Smith and other locals were happy with the assistance they were getting from the workers, but were frustrated with the approach that the team was taking. Although Ms. Smith initially shared her organization's desires with the disaster team, the workers did not heed too much to their requests; not once did they seek their input as the work progressed. It appeared as if Olive Branch had no interest in truly working *with* them and were more interested in working *on* them. In fact, Ms. Smith wondered about their true motive. "Are you really here to help us or is this to advance your own interest and cause?" a frustrated Ms. Smith asked a member of Olive Branch. Earlier that week, an argument had ensued between a member of the disaster team and several community members. The argument was the manifestation of weeks of tension that had been building between the two parties. They were discussing the progress of the work on the community center and the new activity programs that could be added to what was previously offered. Bill felt that since Olive Branch was financing the project, they should have a bigger role in how the money is spent, the style of the building, as well as how the building should be used. As such, they had been passing directives and making decisions about the design of the building without meaningfully engaging Ms. Smith or the people in the community. Any opposition or questions Bill got from the villagers were interpreted as ingratitude. Ms. Smith, having lived through many disasters on the island, especially hurricanes, had clear ideas of how she wanted the building to be rebuilt to mitigate disaster impact. She was aware of the strict building codes that the Government of St. Vincent and the Grenadines had put in place. She also did not want to take shortcuts and just use cheap materials to reduce the building cost, knowing they would compromise the quality of the building. Bill had not considered these things before and even though he understood Ms. Smith's concerns, he was not sure about giving up "control." He left the conversation with feelings of frustration and started reflecting on why he came to St. Vincent and the Grenadines in the first place. He decided to call an emergency meeting with the rest of the team that evening.

Self-Reflexivity

During the emergency meeting, Bill wasted no time to highlight his frustration with the way the project was going. He shared that he could not understand how the people in the community did not show more gratitude for the help they were getting, instead of fighting to have input in everything. Many of the other workers shared similar feelings to Bill and wondered if this was the price to pay for their own progress in the world of disaster recovery. After much deliberation, they agreed that they had to find a way to complete the work, as they also stood to benefit from its completion. They pondered on the question that one of the Vincentians shouted to them – "who is really the expert here?" One of the team members challenged them to evaluate themselves and their approach to the work. In essence, he was asking them to engage in a process of *critical self-reflexivity*. This is the process of discovering and questioning power, social identities, and the construction of knowledge (Comstock et al., 2008). It requires the recognition, understanding, and questioning of systems of power and privilege that are often invisible (Kelly & Bhangal, 2018). This led to a decision to hold a meeting with Ms. Smith and other members of the NCPO to clarify any misunderstanding.

Sharing Perspectives

The following day, Ms. Smith and her team met with Bill and the disaster workers. In the meeting, the Vincentians expressed that they were frustrated by the approach the team was taking. They said it appeared as if they were there to establish their own agenda. They echoed that the failure to meaningfully engage them in decisions about the project is tantamount to the image of a "White savior, descending on a developing country to rescue them from their social and economic ills." Many critical analysts have used this narrative to describe foreign aid, and the Vincentians were well aware of this. They also mentioned that the lack of diversity on the disaster team further amplified this appearance of a "White savior" on a rescue mission. In this humanitarian narrative, "whiteness is associated with progress, power, and higher status," and "those in the global South … have lower capacity for development" (Bian, 2022). Additionally, the international aid community had long been criticized for using the global south as a "laboratory for cashing in on disasters."

The Vincentians echoed that they would feel more appreciated and empowered if they were consulted more intentionally and consistently on each phase of the project. Ms. Smith and her team were looking to build relationships with Olive Branch, not just having a building rebuilt. They expressed that they were grateful for the assistance they were getting to rebuild the center, and by extension the community, but wanted to be included in more decisions. They believed that such a partnership would ensure there is a better product. They had seen in other Caribbean countries how foreign humanitarians were congratulated for their selflessness while little regard was paid to the appropriateness and effectiveness of their work.

Bill and his team appreciated the open and frank feedback from the Vincentians. They would never admit it to them, but they were also benefiting from working on the island. They embarked on this international disaster recovery effort partly because it would help to improve their reputation, thereby positioning them to get more funds to do disaster recovery work. Ultimately, their interest in the work overshadowed the needs of the Vincentians.

Hearing the feedback from the Vincentians, Drew and his team endeavored to change their approach to ensure that the perspectives and desires of the Vincentians were incorporated into each stage of the work. They held regular progress "meetings with them and ensured they were more actively involved in the construction of the building.

In-House Disaster Recovery

Two months later, the project was completed, and the disaster team returned home, equipped with lessons on how to truly work with international communities. The first lesson they learnt was on not allowing their own self-interest to overshadow the needs of those who are vulnerable and oppressed. In other words, the advancement of self-interest should not be the driving force behind advancing the well-being of vulnerable communities. The second lesson was on the importance of listening more to the client or client systems. Community members hold a lot of intimate knowledge about their communities and should therefore be seen as the experts of these communities. Accordingly, they should be seen as partners in disaster recovery. The third lesson was the need for cultural sensitivity training. This will prepare the workers to understand cultural norms and how to engage cross-culturally with minoritized communities both at home and abroad. These lessons prompted Olive Branch to hire a disaster social worker, with an MSW, who would help the team in doing culturally grounded disaster recovery. They realized that it was critical not to amplify the effects of natural disasters on communities by having attitudes, approaches, and practices that are not culturally grounded.

Implications for Practice

Interest convergence, a tenet of CRT, draws attention to the self-interest of dominant, powerful groups. It has implications for the way programs and policies that benefit minoritized groups are implemented. It allows us to ask critical questions about all areas of practice, including humanitarian work in international settings. Although the tenet of interest convergence initially described the experiences of people of color in the US, it is appropriate to extend it to international work done by the US. This is because the US is positioned in a dominant role in the provision of disaster relief. Hence, the image of a dominant culture making decisions that benefit minoritized countries to advance their own self-interest can be applied to international work. Questions such as "how are international aid groups cashing in on disaster work?" helps to explain the nature and extent of US interventions or practices. It may then lead individuals and communities to challenge the nature of the practice and get dominant cultures to prioritize the needs of the minoritized communities that they intend to serve. For example, it can help to explain why some programs are ill-conceived or why there is sometimes a lack of meaningful and sustainable partnerships between minoritized and dominant cultures on projects. Unless the needs of minoritized groups are given priority, efforts put in place to advance them may not be effective.

Discussion Questions

1. What were the converging interests of the people in the northern communities in St. Vincent and the Grenadines and the foreign disaster workers?
2. How did the tenet of interest convergence influence the behavior of the disaster workers?
3. What cases of interest convergence are you aware of in your own communities or across the US?
4. What are some similarities and differences between interest convergence in this case and the ones identified in your own community or across the US?
5. What steps can you take to address interest convergence when it becomes evident?

REFERENCES

Bell, D. A. (1980). Brown v. Board of Education and the interest-convergence dilemma. *Harvard Law Review*, 518–533, 93(3).

Bian, J. (2022). The racialization of expertise and professional non-equivalence in the humanitarian workplace. *International Journal of Humanitarian Action*, 7(1), 3. https://doi.org/10.1186/s41018-021-00112-9

Comstock, D. L., Hammer, T. R., Strentzsch, J., Cannon, K., Parsons, J., et al. (2008). Relational- cultural theory: A framework for bridging relational, multicultural, and social justice competencies. *Journal of Counseling & Development*, 86(3), 279–287.

Delgado, R. & Stefancic, J. (2017). *Critical race theory: An introduction* (3rd ed.). New York, NY: New York University Press.

Kelly, B. T., & Bhangal, N. K. (2018). Life narratives as a pedagogy for cultivating critical self-reflection. *New Directions for Student Leadership*, 2018(159), 41–52.

Shih, D. (2017, April 19). *A theory to better understand diversity, and who really benefits*. NPR. www.npr.org/sections/codeswitch/2017/04/19/523563345/a-theory-to-better-understand-diversity-and-who-really-benefits

Yao, C., & Viggiano, T. (2019). Interest convergence and the commodification of international students and scholars in the United States. *Journal Committed to Social Change on Race and Ethnicity*, 5(1), 82–109.

CASE 4.2

Hoʻokuaʻāina
Reclaiming Land, Culture, and Indigenous Voice to Advance Well-Being

SUSAN L. NAKAOKA

> Hawaiians look to the past for their answers. Society today looks to technology and to the future. We are completely going back to those traditional ways and therein lay the answers.
>
> Dean Wilhem, Hoʻokuaʻāina

Introduction

The dominant narratives in community development practice suggest that Indigenous communities have high rates of social problems, but few strengths. This deficit-based lens ignores the perspectives of people of color and does not acknowledge their assets, resources, and cultural wealth. By centering the voice of Indigenous individuals, in this case, Native Hawaiians,[1] ʻāina-based (land-based) community building provides an innovative and powerful approach to strengths-based practice. An emerging leader in 'Aina-based organizations is Hoʻokuaʻāina, a non-profit farm in Hawai'i that provides a gathering place focused on connection, relationships, and well-being through an array of cultural practices and programming. The Indigenous lens used at this special place embodies the Critical Race Theory (CRT) concept of centering the voice of the other through the use of counter stories that highlight the unique cultural and historical strengths of Native Hawaiian land and people. Faced with common framings of Native Hawaiians as troubled, with high rates of incarceration, substance abuse, and health concerns, this organization has reclaimed the narrative through a counter story that focuses on healing, well-being, and cultural abundance through oral history, relationship-building, and aloha.

Dean and Michele Wilhelm started Hoʻokuaʻāina, an 'āina-based organization based on their deep commitment to caring for 'āina and community. Dean was a teacher who was concerned about his students and their emotional well-being. In 2007, this value of caretaking for people led them to buy a 7.5-acre parcel of land in Maunawili, in Kailua on the island of Oʻahu. The mission was to empower youth to develop life strategies and skills through Hawaiian values-based coaching and the cultivation of kalo (taro). His pedagogical approach is rooted in story-telling, Indigenous narratives and the wisdom of kupuna (elders), a version of Aloha ʻAina that can be seen as critical pedagogy for Native Hawaiians (Kaʻopua et al., 2019): "The time-honored values of reverence for the land ('āina) is reflected in cultural wisdoms or proverbs, history and stories (moʻolelo), chant (oli), and other traditional expressions" (p. 274). By 2013, the couple had gained nonprofit status, in-kind support from the community, and modest financial donations. An initial $60,000 grant from the Consuelo Foundation, which at the time was looking for 'āina-based partners to increase protective factors for at-risk youth, catapulted the organization into the five-year growth period that followed. In 2023, a new state Legacy Land Conservation grant awarded Hoʻokuaʻāina over 116 acres of land in order to continue their work, launching the organization into a new era of growth and community- and 'āina-based programming.

Ho'okua'āina has been successful in growing the quality of its programs, which focus on mentorship and life skills for juvenile-justice involved youth, K-12 education programs and community integration efforts. Notably, its farm capacity and land acquisition are a key part of the story, as they literally reclaim Indigenous land, food production, and method to care for the 'āina by developing its community cultural wealth through methods unique and authentic to them. Centering the voice and ways of knowing of the Indigenous community is key to developing their strategies, strategic planning, and program development.

'Āina-Based Programs

The importance of culture, place, land, and historical context is relevant when serving any population. For Native Hawaiian communities though, these elements are even more crucial to ensuring that an intervention or service is appropriate and effective (Mokuau 2002; Trinidad 2012). Place, in the Native Hawaiian context, for example, can refer to "the process of critical consciousness of historical trauma of one's community, and community knowledge of how to live well and be healthy in one's environment" (Trinidad, 2009, p. 2). Incorporating historical context along with culture is extremely important. Native Hawaiian epistemology, or ways of knowing, is a crucial framework for developing a programmatic approach that can speak more directly to the needs of this population (Trinidad, 2012). Culture, place, and land can be articulated as an intersectional way to uplift the voice of Indigenous people. This can be seen through the concept of Critical Indigenous Pedagogy of Place (CIPP), which when incorporated into community-based work, can "serve as a process and method to motivate youth and young adults to learn about their cultural knowledge, histories, collective values, and healing practices" (Trinidad, 2012, p. 2). By refocusing attention on the ʻāina, Native Hawaiians can begin the healing process from historical trauma. It is through the process of CIPP that the voice of Native Hawaiians can be developed and strengthened to support self-determination.

Aloha ʻāina, sometimes used interchangeably with mālama ʻāina (caring for the land), is a political and programmatic approach that centers relationship with land with cultural understandings of wellbeing and abundance. Aloha ʻāina can be defined as: "the notion that if you take care of the land, the land takes care of you ... the restoration of that reciprocal relationship between Hawaiians and their land, both through political means to regain land rights and through a resurgence of traditional conservation oriented ... land stewardship and subsistence practices" (Gupta, 2015, p. 530). Wright and Balutski (2016) frame aloha ʻāina as crucial to their model of Kanaka ʻŌiwi CRT, describing the importance of land and place as central organizing concepts for Native Hawaiian narratives. In developing KanakaCrit as a decolonizing framework, Reyes (2018) describes how occupation and colonization of land and mind are connected – Native Hawaiian narratives must be re-centered to decolonize thought, self-perception and physical land reclamation. Although non-Indigenous people may imagine this perspective is useful in environmental endeavors but not necessarily helpful in *people* endeavors, there is scholarship that details the use of aloha ʻāina in mental health work. For example, Mokuau (2002) describes how aloha ʻāina substance abuse programs "reflect the Native Hawaiian cosmography that people originate from the land, are stewards of the land, and are recipients of its bounty" (p. 585). She describes that working in kalo terraces (taro patches) has benefits: "Such work entails physical discipline, cognitive attention, emotional reflection, and spiritual openness ... In doing such culturally significant work, participants learn values such as cooperation and reciprocity, engage in self-reflection on cultural identity and cultural pride, and have opportunities to explore their spirituality" (p. 586). Thus, Hoʻokuaʻāina's, programs that use either culturally relevant practices, CIPP or aloha 'āina, can be more impactful due to their ability to connect with the program participants by embracing Hawaiian epistemology and connection to land. These practices can provide benefits to other populations (other Asian Americans, Pacific Islanders, etc.) as well as with Native Hawaiians (Trinidad, 2012).

Culture-Based Programs

The benefits of incorporating culture into prevention and intervention programs has been well documented in literature (Ka'opua et al., 2019; Kim & Jackson, 2009; Mokuau, 2002; Powers, 2006; Uttal, 2006; Yamauchi, 2006). Native Hawaiian cultural strengths may be viewed as protective factors and should be the focus of prevention and treatment efforts (Mokuau, 2002, p. 583). Reese and Vera (2007) studied cultural competence and cultural relevance as integral to developing prevention strategies for mental health programs. They explain, however, that there is not enough literature on how programs successfully integrate culture into their delivery of services or prevention efforts (Reese & Vera, 2007). Specifically, the use of mo'olelo (stories, history) can be an integral tool in social work interventions, especially when the wisdom of elders, or kūpuna, are centered (Ka'opua et al., 2019). One of the program interns stated, "This is the work of the kūpuna. This is a decolonial act itself. When you plant kalo, you are saying that you want a Hawai'i that respects and lives the way our ancestors did."

CRT and Indigenous Voices

CRT scholars have established counter storytelling, the use of narratives from the marginalized, as a technique to uncover racial and colonial oppression in the everyday lives of individuals (Brown & Jackson, 2013). CRT, a framework developed to analyze Native Hawaiian perspectives (Reyes, 2018; Wright & Balutski, 2016), speaks to issues of colonization as endemic to society and to the importance of self-determination and sovereignty of Indigenous knowledge, land, and community development. In developing Kanaka ʻŌiwi CRT, Wright and Balutski (2016) connect the ʻāina to people's conceptions of their own identities and to the stories (moʻolelo) that are important to their lives. Aloha ʻāina can be a process that reinforces Indigenous identity through the creation of narratives tied to the land and to familial connections to stories tied to place. In the case of Hoʻokuaʻāina, Indigenous voices are centered in the reclamation of the land, lessons conveyed through moʻolelo, and the traditional practices related to food production.

Hoʻokuaʻāina Origins and History

Dean, whose father hailed from a farming village in Switzerland, and mother was Native Hawaiian, grew up in the Hawaiian Renaissance, which he describes as "a time when Hawaii rose up to preserve those things that were important. There were connections to the civil rights movement, to anti-Vietnam war protests; there was a feeling that we were going to change things." Indigenous people were asserting their rightful place on the land. Michele, who he met in college, is from a small farming community in Northern California. Her background in landscape architecture and familiarity with farm life, created a perfect partner to build a "collective dream" that became Hoʻokuaʻāina. When the Wilhelms lived in a suburban Oʻahu neighborhood with their young family, they began hosting casual gatherings for others longing for the opportunity to come together, build community, and discuss issues impacting their families. These gatherings revolved around preparing and sharing Hawaiian food often grown in their garden, fellowship, and music. As the gatherings grew, their dream to build a meeting place for community members was born. The couple sold their house, moved their family into a local church, and worked as caretakers while saving money for their vision. In 2007, after three years of searching, they purchased the 7.5 acre parcel of land known as Kapalai in Maunawili, located in Kailua on the windward side of

Oʻahu. The organization gained nonprofit status in 2009, and its early years focused on developing the farm and on nonprofit administration. Dean worked full time, teaching youth in the juvenile justice system and his spare time was spent clearing the land, while Michele focused part time on administration to build the organization. Community engagement was crucial during this period, as many local residents and family friends volunteered to establish the initial wetland-style kalo patches. The central vision of strengthening community bonds and Dean and Michele's commitment created the foundation for a strong mission-driven organization. Restoration and reclamation were key themes mentioned in the interviews.

Organizational Growth

By 2018, the organization had blossomed into a full-fledged working farm with four full-time staff, one part-time education director, and twelve interns at any given time. The flagship mentoring program, Kūkuluhou, for boys in the juvenile justice system, served over 150 boys during this period. Program staff reported positive outcomes, including a reduction in behavioral issues and increased self-esteem among the boys. It now employs a full-time farm manager, a full-time program coordinator, and a part-time education director along with twenty program interns throughout the year.

Evolution of Programs

Dean explains the connection between land and people: "We grow kalo, but we also grow people. We are in the people business." Using Hawaiian traditional methods of growing kalo is not only a reclamation of traditional stories, practices, and customs, but also a means to restore health in living, relationships, and communities. The array of programs has grown to not only serve more people, but to further refine and solidify their culturally based pedagogy, which is largely based on moʻolelo, or storytelling with the use of proverbs; Dean explained, "we never started as an education program, it happened organically. I was working at a youth correctional facility and we worked with Kalo there. Growing kalo, then the eating of food, it is a powerful tool. Mind, body, spirit was connected to build relationships. The first people I mentored here were those transitioning out of prison."

Kūkuluhou Mentoring Program

Based on these ideas, the flagship program, Kūkuluhou, has served over 150 participants since its first contract in 2013. Although Dean remains the lead instructor of the program, the farm manager, education director, and interns have all become more involved in providing mentorship with justice-involved youth. All staff are intentional about modeling a positive work ethic, teamwork, and kuleana (responsibility) to the farm and to each other. The connection to each other is fortified by the relationship with the land; one participant stated, "Just the act of planting and having your feet in the mud is connection."

Internship Program

The internship program has grown in size and scope, having provided over sixty paid internships in five years. Interns are trained in traditional, organic Hawaiian farming methods, which are often a draw for individuals interested in the environment, organic agriculture, and sustainability. Interns are also trained in the "people" part of Hoʻokuaʻāina's model. Thus, the ʻōlelo noʻeau (Indigenous proverbs) that guide the curriculum of the mentoring and education programs also guide the interactions between Dean and the interns. Dean reminds interns about their kuleana (responsibility) as mentors to the youth that come to the farm. Although interns do not necessarily come from at-risk backgrounds, many who are drawn to the role come with histories of trauma, homelessness, mental health needs, and other issues that may have impacted their overall health and well-being. One former intern described the feeling of returning to the farm: "this is my home away from home. My peaceful place."

This is where I wanted to go every day. This is where I can take a deep breath." Interns have experienced dramatic shifts in their life plans as well as within their own personal lives as a result of their work at the farm. In one case, a student changed her plans of attending college on the continent in favor of remaining on Oʻahu to work on the farm and attend college locally. Another intern was previously homeless and describes his involvement in Hoʻokuaʻāina as life-changing. He describes why Dean Wilhelm is so important to his growth at the farm:

> I see him as pretty much another father figure. He's helped me out through a lot of hard times. He's been my mentor. He's the person I would want to model myself most as. He just seems relaxed and at peace . . . talking to him inside the patch, he's always giving words of wisdom, all the time. Something you can use outside of work, something you can use in the real world. Very useful, selfguiding tools, and I have used those tools in my own life. It's amazing. I do appreciate him more than anybody else that I've met so far, he's just awesome, they're an awesome family.

Community Days

Although there are some days off, most Saturdays are community work days at the farm. These have grown in number and regularity since the beginning of the program. In 2023, over 3,700 people from the community visited the farm. For many Native Hawaiian visitors, this experience is one of the few ways to connect to the land in urban Honolulu. One individual brought her Hawaiian language class to the farm and stated how learning the language and participating in the farm were connected, "It's a food idea, and education, environment, health idea. It has a lot to contribute to the greater conversation, which has far-reaching impact."

Education Program

The K12 education program has gone through the most transformation since its beginnings. The curriculum has been formalized, and the education specialist has taken on more responsibility to help develop relationships with the schools and in teaching the lessons when youth come to the farm. Although Dean is still involved in these visits, transferring some of the leadership to the education specialist is part of the succession planning that he has intentionally implemented. Rather than single visits, this program focuses on developing ongoing relationships with a school, so that a relationship with the land can build over time and students can see the taro-growing process from planting to harvesting. In 2022, 1,875 students from nineteen schools participated in this program.

Ho'okua'āina's Strengths

Hoʻokuaʻāina's organizational strengths can be summed up in three main points. The first encompasses its ability to attract and keep people who are committed to the mission and the taro. Because staff and interns feel they are part of the family and that the Wilhelms invest in their growth, there is a high satisfaction rate with the farm as a workplace. Second, the Wilhelms have been adaptable and flexible in tackling program growth; they made tough decisions about how to grow and what projects to take on. Third, relationship building with funders, the board, and community has been a core element that has enabled the organization's survival. Additionally, a learning environment is fostered for all those who come to the farm. People feel valued and gain something from their connection with Hoʻokuaʻāina, so they return and remain connected. In achieving its programmatic goals, the organization's strengths have been related to an approach characterized by values of aloha and 'ohana (family). The Wilhelms view these values as a process or journey, the driving force behind the farm and the operations. All interviewees reiterated how the Wilhelms made them feel welcome and a part of the family. The most common feeling described is that related to the importance of voice – everyone's voice is cherished, heard, acknowledged, and valued.

Hoʻokuaʻāina's Challenges

The challenges are similar to those of any nonprofit. For example, once the seed funding from the Consuelo Foundation was exhausted, securing reliable and consistent funding is an ongoing concern. Organizationally, challenges were found in the areas of rapid growth. The program model relies upon moʻolelo, relationship-building, and intentionality around cultural practices – processes that take time. In other words, rapid growth jeopardized the ability to adhere to the timelines needed to highlight the voices of the community. In addition, the Wilhelms were new to nonprofit administration, so there was a very fast learning process that is ongoing. Because of the quality of the program and its strong reputation, at times it was overwhelming to consider the many options for growth that were encountered. Keeping boundaries between family life and the organization was also difficult. Michele said, "We have to be really deliberate about it. We have been more cautious about programming and about making sure we have evenings and Sundays to ourselves. It doesn't always happen, but we try." Programmatically, measuring the impact of the prevention and community-building functions has been a challenge. New methods and attention to process-oriented outcomes are working, but more development in this area could be helpful.

Although Dean is proactively engaged in succession planning, his ability to develop new leadership is sometimes constrained by competing responsibilities on the farm and demands on his time, given that the voice of the community is widely perceived to be best expressed through his charismatic storytelling methods. Other strategies that were deemed central to success included: strong adherence to mission, inspirational leadership, and connection to the larger decolonization movement of aloha ʻāina practitioners, a focus on growth of people (staff and program participants), an intersectional approach (focus on culture, environment, health and social ties – community cultural wealth), and positive and meaningful relationships with seed funders. All these challenges, in essence, sought to derail the efforts of the program itself in advancing the voice of the people of Hawaiʻi.

Implications for Practice

The program goals of Hoʻokuaʻāina serve to enhance protective factors in the local community. The programming aims to build more support for youth and the broader community. The assumption that "everyone is at risk in some way" reinforces the organization's need to use the seven lessons in all interactions and programs. Three of its four programs are open to everyone (not just at risk youth) and build support within the broader community. To varying degrees, the following protective factors are addressed by the programs and operations of the farm: community connectedness, connection to school, connection to a caring adult, emotional health, equitable access to education and jobs, and embracing cultural attitudes, norms, and values.

There are several examples of how these protective factors are enhanced through the work of Hoʻokuaʻāina. Firstly, community workdays reach thousands of individuals per year. These build on the community connectedness that began in the early days with the initial clearing of the land. Through the community investment of "sweat equity" into the land at the farm, people feel their unique stories are connected to the place and to each other. Dean Wilhelm, the staff, and interns serve as caring adults for the youth that come to the farm. The ongoing relationship between Dean and the Kūkuluhou Mentorship Program participants serves as the heart of the organization. With the increased involvement of the staff and interns, connections with many caring adults are facilitated at the farm. The Education Program and Intern Program provide access to youth and young adults who are actively engaged in education. Through their involvement and work at Hoʻokuaʻāina, the importance of culturally based education is coupled with mainstream education programs. Native Hawaiian cultural knowledge, values, and practices that are established by the program serve as protective factors for youth of all ethnicities.

There is a growing field of community-based programming in Hawaiʻi that uses culture and ʻāina-based approaches to foster youth development, economic development, education, food security, and overall health and well-being. Michele describes this as a movement: "it's way beyond us. It's a movement that's happening in line with a lot of other organizations and the model will be scaling up in the next couple of years." 'Āina Wellness Academy, MA'O Organic Farms, Ho'oulu 'Āina Nature Preserve, and Paepae o He'eia are just a few examples of programs or nonprofits on the island of O'ahu that have helped solidify these vibrant, holistic approaches to 'āina-based development. Ho'okua'āina represents an important contribution to the 'āina-based development field, explicitly combining culture and place-based approaches with relationship building that fosters community bonds as a central focal point – rather than a by-product – of its work, thus centering their community cultural wealth.

The Aloha 'Āina movement is a viable community development method that centers the narrative and voice of Indigenous people of Hawai'i. Their voice, stories, and mo'olelo are the guiding force in the method, as land cannot be separated from family, culture, spirit, and survival. Programs like Ho'okua'āina are part of a larger movement to reclaim land, narrative, self-determination and power. Reclamation of physical space is then connected to occupying space in the historical imaginary of the US in ways that center Indigenous peoples. A future with vibrant Indigenous spaces, with cultural relevance, environmental abundance, cultural wealth, and interconnectedness can be possible; if you visit the 'āina, you can hear the ancestors guide us there.

Discussion Questions

1. Discuss ways in which the community's voice may have been stifled due to historical trauma, occupation, and oppression.
2. How might Indigenous communities, especially those in the Pacific Islands, utilize CRT or Kanaka 'Ōiwi CRT as an analytic frame? In what other ways can communities advance their voices to control their own narratives that shape their histories and future?
3. Although Ho'okua'āina has been on a steady trajectory of growth, are there examples of other Indigenous-centered movements or organizations that

have not been as successful in using these community-based approaches? What might be some of their barriers to success?

4. What ways can you help to advance the voices of marginalized communities, groups, or individuals that you work with?

Note

1 Native Hawaiians are also referred to as Kānaka 'Ōiwi and Kānaka Maoli, which may be the preferred terminology for some Indigenous scholars.

REFERENCES

Blaich, M. D. (2003). Mai uka a i kai: From the mountains to the sea: 'Āina-based education in the ahupua'a of Waipā. Doctoral dissertation, University of Hawaii at Manoa.

Brown, K., & Jackson, D. D. (2013). The history and conceptual elements of critical race theory. In *Handbook of critical race theory in education* (pp. 29–42). Routledge.

Connolly, P. M. (2011). The best of the humanistic and technocratic: Why the most effective work in philanthropy requires a balance. *The Foundation Review, 3*(1), 11.

Fisher-Borne, M., Cain, J. M., & Martin, S. L. (2015). From mastery to accountability: Cultural humility as an alternative to cultural competence. *Social Work Education, 34*(2), 165–181.

Gupta, C. (2015). Return to freedom: Anti-GMO Aloha 'Āina activism on Molokai as an expression of place-based food sovereignty. *Globalizations, 12*(4), 529–544.

Kana'iaupuni, S. M. (2008). He Puko'a Kani 'Aina: Mapping student growth in Hawaiian-focused charter schools. *Journal of American Indian Education, 47*(3), 31–52.

Ka'opua, L. S. I., Friedman, B. D., Duncombe, R., Mataira, P. J., & Bywaters, P. (2019). Indigenous peoples and the social determinants of health. Weaving tradition and innovation to advance health for all. *British Journal of Social Work, 49*(4), 843–853.

Kim, R. J., & Jackson, D. S. (2009). Outcome evaluation findings of a Hawaiian culture-based adolescent substance abuse treatment program. *Psychological Services, 6*(1), 43.

Mokuau, N. (2002). Culturally based interventions for substance use and child abuse among native Hawaiians. *Public Health Reports, 117* (Suppl 1), S82.

Mokuau, N. (2011). Culturally based solutions to preserve the health of Native Hawaiians. *Journal of Ethnic & Cultural Diversity in Social Work, 20*(2), 98–113.

Mokuau, N., Garlock-Tuiali'i, J., & Lee, P. (2008). Has social work met its commitment to Native Hawaiians and other Pacific Islanders? A review of the periodical literature. *Social Work, 53*(2), 115–121.

Powers, K. M. (2006). An exploratory study of cultural identity and culture-based educational programs for urban American Indian students. *Urban Education, 41*(1), 20–49.

Reese, L. R. E., & Vera, E. M. (2007). Culturally relevant prevention: The scientific and practical considerations of community-based programs. *The Counseling Psychologist, 35*(6), 763–778.

Reyes, N. A. S. (2018). A space for survivance: Locating Kānaka Maoli through the resonance and dissonance of critical race theory. *Race, Ethnicity and Education, 21*(6), 739–756.

Trinidad, A. M. (2009). Toward *kuleana* (responsibility): A case study of a contextually grounded intervention for Native Hawaiian youth and young adults. *Aggression and Violent Behavior, 14*(6), 488–498.

Trinidad, A. M. (2012). Critical indigenous pedagogy of place: A framework to indigenize a youth food justice movement. *Journal of Indigenous Social Development, 1*(1A).

Trust-Based Philanthropy Network. https://trustbasedphilanthropy.org/?fbclid=IwAR1Mzb1Q1AQ3KTmOu_GZ62E8pI6RFJj7IdXRMZN1iclwiG-PVefAZ2qpQuY

Uttal, L. (2006). Organizational cultural competency: Shifting programs for Latino immigrants from a client-centered to a community-based orientation. *American Journal of Community Psychology, 38*(3–4), 201–212.

Wright, E. K. A., & Balutski, B. J. N. (2016). Ka 'Ikena a ka Hawai'i: Toward a Kanaka 'Ōiwi critical race theory. In B. J. N. Balutski et al. (Eds.), *Kanaka 'Ōiwi methodologies: Mo 'olelo and metaphor* (pp. 86–108). University of Hawaii Press.

Yamauchi, L. A. (2003). Making school relevant for at-risk students: The Wai'anae High School Hawaiian Studies Program. *Journal of Education for Students Placed at Risk, 8*(4), 379–390.

Yosso, T. J. (2005). Whose culture has capital? A critical race theory discussion of community cultural wealth. *Race Ethnicity and Education, 8*(1), 69–91.

CASE 4.3

Advancing the Voices of Those Who Are Marginalized
A Macro Intervention to Prevent Dating Violence and Intersecting Racial and Sexual Identity Disparities in New Mexico

ANNA N. NELSON

Laying a Foundation

Constance-Huggins (2012) and Kolivoski et al. (2014) name advancing the voices of those who are marginalized as a core tenet of critical race theory (CRT)-grounded social work practice. This tenet centers the cultural capital, community cultural wealth, and lived expertise (Kolivoski et al., 2014; Yosso, 2005) of Black, Indigenous and People and Communities of Color as valid and valuable sources of knowledge (Ladson-Billings, 1998). Advancing the voices of those who have been directly impacted by racism and oppression challenges dominant perspectives on the existence of racism (Kolivoski et al., 2014, p. 271) and the normalization of stereotypes that validate oppression in the United States (Yosso, 2005). Authentically advancing these voices begins with accepting that lived experiences with racism and intersecting oppression are daily truths for Black, Indigenous and People and Communities of Color. Honoring their counter stories of strength, perseverance and collective healing in the face of adversity is equally important. Finally, valuing the family histories and cultural traditions shared across generations (Ladson-Billings, 1998; Solórzano & Yosso, 2001) of those who experience marginalization is vital.

This macro case study tells a counter story of one social worker's campaign to eliminate dating violence and intersecting disparities (Roberts et al., 2018) after the loss of a young client to homicide in New Mexico. Her prevention efforts were focused on uplifting the voices of Black, Indigenous, Latine and Youth of Color (BILYC) and Lesbian, Gay, Bisexual, Transgender, Queer, Questioning, Intersex, Asexual, and Two Spirit+ (LGBTQQIA2S+) youth who were impacted by dating violence. The case study describes antiracist positive youth engagement and community participatory action methods the social worker employed to achieve policy transformation that meaningfully and sustainably reduced rates of dating violence statewide. Social work students are encouraged to explore the discussion questions to develop their own antiracist action steps for future practice.

Dating Violence and Intersecting Ethnic and Sexual Identity Inequities

Dating violence, or acts of physical, sexual, psychological or emotional abuse, violence, stalking, and harassment against a current or former dating or intimate partner between the ages of twelve and eighteen years (National Institute of Justice, n.d.), is a critical public health issue nationwide. Dating violence is correlated with a sequelae of preventable health outcomes for young people, including early, unplanned pregnancy (Silverman et al., 2001), rapid repeat pregnancy within twenty-four months of giving birth (Jacoby et al., 1999), as well as depression and increased risk for suicide (Gasperecz et al., 2023; Olshen et al., 2007; Piolanti et al., 2023;). It is also associated with substance use (Piolanti et al., 2023; Rostad et al., 2020), emotional trauma (Jouriles et al., 2017), risk for being victimized by (Jouriles et al., 2017) or perpetrating adult intimate partner violence (Taquette & Montiero, 2019), and becoming victims of homicide (Adhia et al., 2019).

Black, Indigenous, Latine and Youth of Color (BILYC) and LGBTQQIA2S+ youth are at significantly greater risk for dating violence exposure and subsequent adverse health and social outcomes (Clayton et al., 2023; Roberts et al., 2018). While contending with exposure to trauma from dating violence, BILYC and LGBTQQIA2S+ youth are simultaneously exposed to racism, homophobia, and transphobia, where racism (Williams et al., 2018), sexism (Kucharska, 2018), and homophobia (Valentine et al., n.d.) are also directly correlated with risk for cumulative traumatic effect (Nelson, 2022). These inequities reflect the intersections of racial and sexual identity and structural racism and oppression as drivers of adverse health outcomes (Roberts et al., 2018). Exposure to ethnoracial and other oppression-based trauma disrupts positive racial identity development (Svetaz et al., 2020) and creates a sense of not belonging (Akbulut & Razum, 2022). Trauma exposure can also profoundly change a person's sense of self (Lanius et al., 2020), core beliefs, sense of belonging (Wilde, 2022), self-worth (Li & Liang, 2023) and sense of mattering.

Physical dating violence prevalence among New Mexico's high school students in 2021 was 9.4 percent (Centers for Disease Control and Prevention, 2021). However, in 2007, the prevalence of physical dating violence for New Mexico's high school students was significantly higher than the national rate at 12.6 percent (Eaton et al., 2008; New Mexico Department of Health, 2015). Rates of dating violence declined to between 8.6 percent and 9.4 percent in the following eight years, remaining comparable to the national prevalence.

Whereas New Mexico's rate of physical dating violence remained stable and commensurate with national prevalence in recent years, prevalence for BILYC, LGBTQQI2S+ youth, and high school students born outside the US remain significantly higher than their White, straight, cisgender, US-born peers. In 2015, 9.4 percent of American Indian/Alaska Native, 18.6 percent of Asian/Pacific Islander, 16 percent of Black, and 8.2 percent of Latine students reported experiencing physical dating violence, compared with their White peers at 8.1 percent (New Mexico Department of Health, 2015). Also, 22 percent of students who identified as gay or lesbian and 21 percent of bisexual students reported experiencing dating violence, compared with their straight peers at 6.6 percent (New Mexico Department of Health, 2015). Further disparities were noted for students who were born outside the US, at 15.9 percent, compared with all high school students at 8.9 percent (New Mexico Department of Health, 2015). These disparities echo 2021 findings from the national Youth Risk Behavior Survey, where inequities in dating violence occurred for some ethnic and sexual minority students by type of violence (Clayton et al., 2023), particularly for American Indian/Alaska Native, multiracial, and lesbian, gay and bisexual students.

From Devastating Loss to Social Transformation: A Macro Case Study Uplifting the Voices of Black, Indigenous, Latine and Youth of Color to End Dating Violence

Mia, a crisis response social worker, received a request to provide family support services to a Latine family living in a working-class

Community of Color in New Mexico. When Mia first met with the family, she learned that the grandparents recently began raising their grandchildren after a parental traumatic loss and incarceration of a relative who was previously the children's guardian. One of the grandchildren in the family was a fourteen-year-old named Gabriela. Gabriela appeared quiet and withdrawn, had run away on several occasions, was experiencing difficulties with her peers at school, was frequently truant, and appeared hyper-protective of her privacy and cell phone use. Though Mia shared many cultural and linguistic similarities with the family, she had trouble building a rapport with Gabriella, who was mistrustful and apprehensive of Mia's attempts to engage with her. Because Gabriela and her family experienced significant traumatic losses, Mia made a referral to specialized trauma treatment through another community-based organization. Soon after the family was transferred, Mia received a call saying that Gabriela had been murdered.

During the homicide investigation, police discovered that Gabriela was in a relationship with an adult male who controlled her and became violent if she spent time with her friends and family. Though Mia was skilled in identifying warning signs for adults experiencing intimate partner violence and children who witnessed parental violence, Gabriela's cries for help as a young victim of dating violence went undetected. Deeply impacted by this loss, Mia began a journey to better understand signs and indicators for young people experiencing dating violence, how many young people were impacted, and what could be done to end dating violence in New Mexico.

During this timeframe, nearly a quarter (23 percent or five deaths) of all intimate partner violence-related homicides in New Mexico involved adolescents under age eighteen (New Mexico Intimate Partner Violence Death Review Team, 2009). By conducting a literature review of dating violence nationally and exploring New Mexico-specific youth risk survey data, Mia quickly identified that bullying and technology abuse were two dating-violence specific tactics for control, both strategies used against Gabriela. Mia learned that Latinas – like Gabriela – Black, and Indigenous girls (Roberts et al.,

2018) experienced physical and sexual dating violence more frequently than their White peers. The research also showed correlations between dating violence and increased risk for youth substance use, depression and suicide, early, unplanned and rapid repeat pregnancy, where New Mexico shared the highest rate of teen pregnancy nationally with Texas in 2006 (Worthington, 2008).

This research guided the development of a logic model to define data-driven strategic action steps Mia and community members could take to prevent dating violence. Also, as a youth-serving social worker, Mia developed a community asset map to guide her outreach to colleagues working in community-based organizations focused on youth violence, early, unplanned pregnancy, bullying, suicide, and substance use prevention. These relationships provided access for Mia to share data-driven information and resources directly with community providers and young people, resulting in the training of more than 500 people in a year.

Although this was a good start, collective action was needed to bring dating violence prevention directly to young people. Mia understood the power of positive youth development approaches that centered racial identity (Lantos et al., 2022) and youth-led peer education as ways for both uplifting marginalized voices of Black, Indigenous, Latine and LGBTQQIA2S+ youth and honoring their lived experiences as legitimate and valued. Mia began to engage cadres of youth peer educators statewide, many of whom were trained in school-based suicide prevention. These young people were committed to providing culturally and identity-grounded education and resources to their peers on signs of dating violence and skills for building healthy relationships. However, in some areas of the state, these efforts were seen as impinging on parental rights, leading some school districts to refuse participation.

This significant systems barrier needed a policy-level solution. Mia began to develop relationships with policymakers nationally, including legislative aids serving Senator Mike Crapo from Idaho and Senator Hillary Rodham Clinton in New York, who assisted her in crafting a legislative proclamation naming the first week in February

2008, *Teen Dating Violence Awareness and Prevention Week*. Signed by Governor Bill Richardson on January 14, 2008, this proclamation marked the first of its kind in the state and empowered prevention specialists and youth peer educators to provide dating violence awareness information in schools across New Mexico.

From this proclamation and legislative advocacy, the 2009 New Mexico House Memorial 53: Prevention of Teen Dating Violence Study, co-led by the New Mexico Department of Health Office of School and Adolescent Health and Public Education Department, was enacted. Acting as co-facilitator of this study, Mia ensured young people were at the table during the study and engaged youth from Tribes, Pueblos and Communities of Color statewide. Five youth-led community dialogues with Spanish-speaking youth, youth who were immigrants, young people from the Navajo Nation, Acoma and Laguna Pueblos, and members of the Office of African American Affairs were convened. Questions posed to the young people who participated in these dialogues included:

1) What are the forms of dating violence you have experienced first-hand or observed with your friends?
2) Who would you trust to go to for support if you were in a violent dating relationship?
3) What are the red flags of dating violence?
4) What do you think adults need to understand about dating violence?; and
5) What services or resources are needed to stay safe from dating violence?

This study resulted in a full report and robust recommendations that were collaboratively developed, inclusive of responses from the youth community dialogues, and vetted by community partners.

The report and recommendations targeted action steps for the New Mexico State Legislature, Department of Health, Public Education Department, Children, Youth and Families Department, and Behavioral Health Collaborative. A significant recommendation stemming from this study was the need for funding to eliminate behavioral health resource disparities for Black people statewide. The study also emphasized the importance of uplifting cultural capital and community cultural wealth as promotive of health and well-being for Black, Indigenous, and Latine youth.

This study played a prominent role in legislation requiring health education as a graduation requirement for all high school students statewide. Finally, in response to an increase in dating violence-related homicides involving Native American, Latine, and immigrant adolescents statewide, a Teen Dating Violence committee of the New Mexico Intimate Partner Violence Death Review Team at the University of New Mexico was established (New Mexico Intimate Partner Violence Death Review Team, 2010). This institutionalized the analysis of intersecting systems inequities and failures that contributed to dating violence homicides.

During this period, through the collective efforts of community-based youth-serving organizations, youth peer educators and leaders from Black, Indigenous and Latine communities, and schools statewide, New Mexico went from ranking in the top ten states nationally with the highest rates of dating violence to thirty-first in the nation (Centers for Disease Control and Prevention, 2010). While the state's overall dating violence prevalence continues to be at or below the national average, culturally and identity- grounded prevention practices and structural interventions remain vital in addressing inequitable impact of dating violence for Black, Indigenous, Latine, and LGBTQQIA2S+ youth in New Mexico and nationally.

What Happens When Voices of Those Who Are Marginalized Are Not Advanced? Practice Implications

Social work is one of a handful of professions predicated on social justice, where social workers are ethically compelled to advocate for human rights and racial justice by intentionally integrating antiracism, diversity, equity, and inclusion at "individual, family, group, organizational, and community systems levels" (Council on Social

Work Education, 2022, p. 9). To dismantle the dual legacies of structural racism and White supremacy, the profession received a call to action to eliminate racism as a Social Work Grand Challenge (Teasley et al., 2021). The grand challenge of eliminating racism and intersecting oppression cannot be achieved without centering the voices of BILYC, LGBTQQIA2S+ Youth, and Communities of Color as experts in their experiences with racism and oppression and innovators in strategies for ending structural and institutional inequities. By advancing the voices of those who are marginalized, social workers promote a sense of mattering through validation (Strayhorn, 2008), authentic care for the dignity and worth of those they are serving, and an expressed commitment to the advancement of Communities of Color and communities that are marginalized (Palmer & Maramba, 2012). For social workers to not actively engage in antiracist action is to be part of the problem.

Svetaz et al. (2020) define antiracism as people taking collective action across a diversity of cultures, identities, languages, lived experiences, and spiritual beliefs "to change systems or institutional policies, practices or procedures that have racists effects" (p. 323). The authors define a clear antiracist, anti-oppressive framework easily adoptable by social workers, including "activation," or focusing on advancing the voices of people who are marginalized, using antiracist, non-stigmatizing language, as well as promoting awareness and education on antiracism. It also includes building coalitions and alliances through participatory action, honoring traditional knowledge and ways of healing, and actively engaging in advocacy and critical reflectivity (Svetaz et al., 2020, p. 324). Mia's journey to prevent dating violence in New Mexico by centering the voices of BILYC and LGBTQQIA2S+ and engaging in collaborative participatory action elucidates how this framework can be applied in everyday social work macro practice.

Discussion Questions

1. Using Svetaz et al.'s (2020) antiracist, anti-oppressive framework, what is one step you can take to integrate antiracism, diversity, equity and inclusion in

your everyday practices and practicum experiences? How can you take measures to advance the voices of marginalized people you serve?

2. How can you actively advance the voices of Black, Indigenous, Latino, and LGBTQQIA2S+ youth in your social work practice? What strategies would you use to ensure that voices not equitably reflected are included?

3. What macro-level skills can you identify for engagement, assessment, and intervention to enhance dating violence prevention at both the community and state levels?

4. Identify how you would use research to enhance your prevention efforts. What specific research methods or findings could you use to advance equity and racial justice in your work?

REFERENCES

Adhia, A., Kernic, M. A., Hemenway, D., Vavilala, M. S., & Rivara, F. P. (2019). Intimate partner homicide of adolescents. *Journal of the American Medical Association, 173*(6), 571-577. https://doi.org/10.1001/jamapediatrics.2019.0621

Akbulut, N., & Razum, O. (2022). Why othering should be considered in research on health inequalities: Theoretical perspectives and research needs. *Social Sciences & Medicine Population Health Journal, 20,* 101286. https://doi.org10.1016/j.ssmph.2022.101286

Clayton, H. B., Klimer, G., DeGue, S., Estefan, L. F., Le, V. D., Suarez, N. A., Lyons, B. H., & Thornton, J. E. (2023). Dating violence, sexual violence, and bullying victimization among high school students: Youth Risk Behavior Survey, United States, 2021. Centers for Disease Control and Prevention Morbidity and Mortality Weekly Report. www.cdc.gov/mmwr/volumes/72/su/su7201a8.htm

Centers for Disease Control and Prevention. (2010). Morbidity and mortality weekly report: Youth risk behavior surveillance, United States, 2009. www.cdc.gov/mmwr/pdf/ss/ss5905.pdf

Centers for Disease Control and Prevention. (2021). High school youth risk behavior survey: New Mexico 2021 and United States 2021 Results. www.cdc.gov/healthyyouth/data/yrbs/results.htm

Constance-Huggins, M. (2012). Critical Race Theory in social work education: A framework for addressing racial disparities. *Critical Social Work, 12*(2), 1-16. www.uwindsor.ca/criticalsocialwork/criticalracetheoryinsocialwork education

Council on Social Work Education. (2022). 2022 Educational policy and accreditation standards for baccalaureate and master's social work programs. Council on Social Work Education. www.cswe.org/getmedia/bb5d8afe-7680-42dc-a332-a6e6103f4998/2022-EPAS.pdf

Eaton, D. K., Kann, L., Kinchen, S., Shanklin, S., Ross, J., Harris, W. A., Lowry, R., McManus, T., Chyen, D., Lim, C., Brener, N. D., & Weschler, H. (2008). Youth risk behavior surveillance – United States, 2007. Centers for Disease Control and Prevention. www.cdc.gov/mmwr/preview/mmwrhtml/ss5704a1.htm#:~:text=Overall%2C%20the%20prevalence%20of%20dating, (10.1%25)%20students%2C%20respectively

Gasperecz, J. W., Baumler, E., Wood, L., & Temple, J. R. (2023). Suicidal ideation and psychological dating violence victimization: A short report. *Frontiers in Psychiatry, 14*, 1–4. https://doi.org/10.3389/fpsyt.2023.1105654

Jacoby, M., Gorenflo, D., Black, E., Wonderlich, C., & Eyler, A. E. (1999). Rapid repeat pregnancy and experiences of interpersonal violence among low-income adolescents. *American Journal of Preventative Medicine, 16*(4), 318–321. https://doi.org/10.1016/s0749-3797(99)00029-x

Jouriles, E. N., Choi, H. J., Rancher, C., & Temple, J. R. (2017). Teen dating violence victimization, trauma symptoms and re-victimization in early adulthood. *Journal of Adolescent Health, 61*(1), 115–119. https://doi.org/10.1016/j.jadohealth.2017.01.020

Kolivoski, K. M., Weaver, A., & Constance-Huggins, M. (2014). Critical Race Theory: Opportunities for application in social work practice and policy. *Families in Society, 95*(4), 269–276. https://doi.org/10.1606/1044-3894.2014.95.36

Kucharska, J. (2018). Cumulative trauma, gender discrimination and mental health in women: Mediating role of self-esteem. *Journal of Mental Health, 27*(5), 416–423. https://pubmed.ncbi.nlm.nih.gov/29260963/

Ladson-Billings, G. (1998) Just what is critical race theory and what's it doing in a nice field like education? *International Journal of Qualitative Studies in Education, 11*(1), 7–24. https://doi.org/10.1080/095183998236863

Lanius, R. A., Terpou, B. A., & McKinnon, M. C. (2020). The sense of self in the aftermath of trauma: Lessons from the default mode network in posttraumatic stress disorder. *European Journal of Psychotraumatology, 11*. https://doi.org/10.1080/20008198.2020.1807603

Lantos, H., Allen, T., Abdi, F. M. Franco, F., Moore, K. A., Snell, J., Bruce, B., Redd, Z., Robuck, R., & Miller, J. (2022). Integrating positive youth development and racial equity, inclusion and belonging approaches across the child welfare and justice systems. Child Welfare. www.childtrends.org/

publications/integrating-positive-youth-development-and-racial-equity-inclusion-and-belonging-approaches-across-the-child-welfare-and-just ice-systems

Li, Y., & Liang, Y. (2023). The effects of childhood trauma on complex posttraumatic stress disorder: The role of self-esteem. *The European Journal of Psychotraumatology, 14*(2). https://doi.org/10.1080/20008066.2023.2272478

McNaughton Reyes, H. L., Foshee, V. A., Tharp, A. T., Ennett, S. T., & Bauer, D. J. (2015). Substance use and physical dating violence: The role of contextual moderators. *American Journal of Preventative Medicine, 49*(3), 467–475. https://doi.org/10.1016/j.amepre.2015.05.018

National Institute of Justice. (n.d.). Teen dating violence. https://nij.ojp.gov/topics/crimes/teen-dating-violence

Nelson, A. N. (2022). Introducing critical trauma theory for black, indigenous and latine/afro-latine students studying social work: A phenomenology of cultural capital in the U.S. Southwest. ProQuest. http://libezp.nmsu.edu:2048/login?url=https://www.proquest.com/dissertations-theses/introducing-critical-trauma-theory-black/docview/2681016178/se-2

Nelson, A. N., & Kew, K. (2023). Riotous research: A Critical Trauma Theory to uplift the language of those unheard Black, Indigenous and Social Work Students of Color. In L. Abrams, S. Edmonds Crewe, A. J. Dettlaff, & J. H. Williams (Eds.), *Social work, white supremacy, and racial justice: Reckoning with our history, interrogating our present, reimagining our future.* Oxford: Oxford University Press. https://doi.org/10.1093/oso/9780197641422.003.0032

New Mexico Department of Health. (2015). New Mexico's health indicator data & statistics: Injury – youth physical dating violence. https://ibis.doh.nm.gov/indicator/summary/InjuryYouthPhysDatingViol.html

New Mexico Department of Health & Public Education Department. (2009). Report on House Memorial (HM) 53: Prevention of teen dating violence. Available upon request at annelson@nmhu.edu.

New Mexico Intimate Partner Violence Death Review Team. (2009). Annual report 2009: Findings and recommendations from calendar year 2006 intimate partner violence deaths. https://hsc.unm.edu/medicine/departments/emergency-medicine/programs/cipre/cipre-programs/ipvdrt/

New Mexico Intimate Partner Violence Death Review Team. (2010). Annual report 2010: Findings and recommendations from calendar year 2007 intimate partner violence deaths. https://hsc.unm.edu/medicine/departments/emergency-medicine/programs/cipre/cipre-programs/ipvdrt/

Olshen, E., McVeigh, K. H., & Wunsch-Hitzig, R. A. (2007). Dating violence, sexual assault, and suicide attempts among urban teenagers. *Archives of*

Pediatrics and Adolescent Medicine, 161(6), 539–545. https://doi.org/10.1001/archpedi.161.6.539

Palmer, R. T., & Maramba, D. C. (2012). Creating conditions of mattering to enhance persistence for Black men at an historically Black university. *Spectrum: A Journal on Black Men, 1*(1), 95–119. https://doi.org/10.2979/spectrum.1.1.95

Piolanti, A., Walker, F., Schmid, I. E., & Foran, H. M. (2023). Long-term adverse outcomes associated with teen dating violence: A systematic review. *Pediatrics, 151*(6). https://doi.org/10.1542/peds.2022-059654

Roberts, L., Tamene, M., & Orta, O. R. (2018). The intersectionality of racial and gender discrimination among teens exposed to dating violence. *Ethnicity & Disease, 28*(Supp. 1), 253–260. https://doi.org/10.18865/ed.28.S1.253

Rostad, W. L., Clayton, H. B., Estefan, L. F., & Johns, M. M. (2020). Substance use and disparities in teen dating violence victimization by sexual identity among high school students. *Prevention Science Journal, 21*(3), 398–407. https://doi.org/10.1007/s11121-019-01049-7

Silverman, J. G., Raj, A., Mucci, L. A., & Hathaway, J. E. (2001). Dating violence against adolescent girls and associated substance use, unhealthy weight control, sexual risk behavior, pregnancy, and suicidality. *Journal of the American Medical Association, 28*(65), 572–579. https://doi.org/10.1001/jama.286.5.572

Solórzano, D. & Yosso, T. (2001) Critical race and LatCrit theory and method: Counterstorytelling Chicana and Chicano graduate school experiences. *International Journal of Qualitative Studies in Education, 14*(4), 471–495. https://doi.org/10.1080/09518390110063365

Strayhorn, T. L. (2008). The role of supportive relationships in facilitating African American males' success in college. *National Association of School Psychologists Journal, 45*(1), 26–48. https://doi.org/10.2202/1949-6605.1906

Svetaz, M. V., Barral, R., Kelley, M. A., Simpson, T., Chulani, V., Raymond-Flesch, M., Coyne-Beasley, T., Trent, M., Ginsburg, K., & Kanbur, N. (2020). Inaction is not an option: Using antiracism approaches to address health inequities and racism and respond to current challenges affecting youth. *Journal of Adolescent Health, 67*(3), 323–325. https://doi.org/10.1016/j.jadohealth.2020.06.017

Taquette, S. R., & Montiero, D. L. (2019). Causes and consequences of adolescent dating violence: A systematic review. *Journal of Injury and Violence Research, 11*(2), 137–147. https://doi.org/10.5249/jivr.v11i2.1061

Teasley, M. L., McCarter, S., Woo, B., Conner, L., Spencer, M. S., & Green, T. (2021). The grand challenge to eliminate racism. Grand Challenges for

Social Work Initiative. https://grandchallengesforsocialwork.org/wp-content/uploads/2021/05/Eliminate-Racism-Concept-Paper.pdf

Teixeira, S., Augsberger, A., Richards-Schuster, K., Martinez, L. S., & Evans, K. (2021). Opportunities to "make macro matter" through the grand challenges for social work. *Families in Society: The Journal of Contemporary Social Services, 102*(3), 414–426. https://doi.org/10.1177/1044389420972488

University of New Mexico Health Sciences Center. (2008). Domestic and sexual violence related homicides in New Mexico: A 2008 annual report of the New Mexico Domestic Violence Homicide Review Team and review of 2005 homicides. https://isr.unm.edu/centers/new-mexico-statistical-analysis-center/ipvdrt/reports/annual-reports/2008-annual-report.pdf

United States Census Bureau. (2020). New Mexico: 2020 census. www.census.gov/library/stories/state-by-state/new-mexico-population-change-between-census-decade.html

Valentine, S. E., Livingston, N. A., Salomaa, A. C., & Shipherd, J. C. (n.d.). Trauma, discrimination and post-traumatic stress disorder among lesbian, gay, bisexual, transgender and queer+ people. US Department of Veterans Affairs. www.ptsd.va.gov/professional/treat/specific/trauma_discrimination_lgbtq.asp

Wilde, L. (2022). Background feelings of belonging and psychological trauma. *Psychopathology, 55*, 191–200. https://doi.org/10.1159/000518327

Williams, M. T., Metzger, I. W., Leins, C., & DeLapp, C. (2018). Assessing racial trauma within a DSM-5 framework: The UConn Racial/Ethnic Stress & Trauma Survey. *Practice Innovations, 3*(4), 242–260. http://dx.doi.org/10.1037/pri0000076

Worthington, A. (2008). New Mexico epidemiology: Highlights of New Mexico vital statistics, 2006. New Mexico Department of Health. www.nmhealth.org/data/view/report/557/

Yosso, T. (2005). Whose culture has capital? A critical race theory discussion of community cultural wealth. *Race, Ethnicity, and Education, 8*(1), 69–91. https://doi.org/10.1080/1361332052000341006

CASE 4.4

The Great Divide
A Neighborhood's Quest of Racial Lines and Property Lines

ZADONNA M. SLAY

This case highlights the critical race theory (CRT) tenet, the critique of liberalism, specifically color-blindness. Color-blindness suggests that since color should not matter, it does not matter in today's society. That is, it does not play a role in shaping outcomes. This ideology overlooks the systemic inequalities and historical injustices that shape social dynamics.

Community Overview

Crosby Heights is a new 152-lot single-family home subdivision that spans ninety-six acres and is near the county line of the City of River Moss. The subdivision was planned in four development stages over six years by the developer and builder, Crimson Clay Builders. The homes range from 1,650 square feet (about half of a tennis court area) to 3,000 square feet (about the area of a tennis court). The starting price for the homes is $225,000. Situated near the county line, the neighborhood is often not considered within the city limits because of the rural environment that surrounds it. There is a gas convenience store and a liquor store within walking distance. The nearest grocery store, fast food, and restaurants are approximately four miles from the subdivision. Moreover, two manufacturing companies neighbor the homes, and a railroad track runs behind the newly built subdivision.

River Moss is the third-largest city in the region and one of the fastest growing in population. According to the last census report, there were approximately 38,000 residents (47 percent male, 53 percent women) with a median age of twenty-nine years old. The racial/ethnic composition of River Moss is 86 percent White (Non-Hispanic), 6 percent Black, 3 percent two or more races, 2 percent White (Hispanic), 1 percent Asian, 0.61 percent Other, 0.48 percent Native Hawaiian/Pacific Islander, and 0.22 percent Native American. The community exhibits an emphasis on work ethic in industries such as manufacturing, agriculture, and quarrying; 48 percent of the residents have a high school diploma or higher, resulting in a low unemployment rate (3 percent), and the majority of residents working in blue-collar careers (65 percent), while 35 percent are working in white-collar jobs. The median household income is $49,000. At present, 60 percent of the population are renters, and 40 percent are homeowners. This new residential development provides housing options for prospective homeowners and expands housing availability in River Moss.

Homeowner's Association Development

The Homeowner's Association (HOA) is a non-profit governing body that enforces the covenants, maintains common spaces, oversees the collection and accounting of the annual HOA fees and other monies, and ensures the organization is legally compliant with state and local regulations. The developer, Crimson Clay Builders, created the HOA. The owner and operator of Crimson Clay Builders, Larry Lee, became the declarant of the Crosby Heights HOA. A declarant is responsible for establishing and creating the HOA's bylaws and covenants.

Mr. Lee appointed residents to join him on the board of directors. He maintained oversight and presided over the HOA until Crosby Heights was 75 percent full (or phase four is halfway complete). The following election, after the subdivision was 75 percent full, Larry transferred all documents and possession of the HOA to the residents for a community-governed HOA board of directors. As the newly appointed HOA board of directors settled into their positions, there was one thing in common – they had never lived in a subdivision with an HOA. They didn't know what to expect, what to ask, or how to anticipate potential challenges.

Since the formulation of the board of directors, there has been a high turnover among its members. The HOA board is all White, the majority being men, with no more than two positions being women. It is typical for a director to not complete their term or serve beyond their first term. The HOA has been unable to enforce the covenants, manage green spaces, clearly define roles and responsibilities for each board member, provide opportunities for regular community engagement, or resolve conflict among the board members and conflict between the board members and residents. The board of directors has solicited the advice of an attorney for support on how to function beyond a "social group." However, residents and the board of directors are unwilling to support or attend meetings to enact change. Directors are too busy with work and family obligations. Residents of Crosby Heights have stated that the meeting time and location are hindrances to attending. Persons have also stated "they don't see the point" of attending the HOA meetings. There tends to be bickering and conflict in the Facebook group for Crosby Heights.

Residents created the group as a space for networking and information sharing. Although social media can be a source of positive community engagement, disagreements can also ensue. The board of directors is unable to be a voice of collaboration and compromise. Collectively, the members do not provide transparent communication or provide opportunities for information sharing. They do not encourage open dialogue or seek to understand different viewpoints. It's simply "their way or the highway."

With time, residents have grown increasingly frustrated with the HOA not being enforced. Several households have stopped paying their annual dues. Residents are tired of race-baiting and fearmongering on social media platforms. This involves communication that only targets persons of color as suspicious persons and alarmist messaging without supporting data, thus leading to negative stereotypes. The HOA officers routinely do not respond to general questions of residents. The president and vice president often miss scheduled neighborhood meetings. When there are neighborhood meetings, the meetings begin late with no agenda and last for hours with no directed outcomes or resolutions. The lawyer for the HOA has maintained that there is nothing that can be done until the developer, Larry Lee, turns his portion of ownership over to the HOA board. However, Mr. Lee has communicated that he has fulfilled his obligation to build the homes, transitioned the HOA to the residents, and is no longer required to participate with the HOA. The president of the HOA shares with the neighborhood group on Facebook that he is doing the best that he can in his role because he is busy with his job and wants to spend time with his family, not tend to neighborhood affairs. The HOA officers contend that they are efficient in their roles because they have compiled annual quotes for lawn maintenance of common areas in Crosby Heights. As a result, the attorney for the HOA has recommended that the board work with a community engagement specialist who is a master-level social worker with a macro practice interest in community/neighborhood development.

Conflict Caused by Colorblindness

Crosby Heights reflects the population of the City of River Moss. The subdivision is primarily White, with a small percentage of persons of color or mixed race. The HOA has not developed and maintained a neighborhood census and does not maintain residents' demographic information. Despite the occasional social media arguments, there's a perception of strong social ties through Food Truck events, community yard sales, and social engagement activities such as trick-or-treating and fireworks. The social events are not sponsored or orchestrated by the HOA. Instead, they are organized by residents who want to create kid-friendly activities or create a social community among neighbors. Overall, there appears to be self-governing as it relates to the covenants of the neighborhood. Questions frequently arise among community members regarding the appropriate methods for monitoring and reporting on the covenants established by the HOA. Residents often seek clarification on the purpose of these covenants, particularly if there appears to be a lack of enforcement by the HOA, leading to concerns about their effectiveness in maintaining community standards and property values. Many residents wish to do away with the HOA as they do not see the need for it. Crime is minimal in the neighborhood. There have been reports of deliveries being stolen from porches but no reports of breaking and entering homes and automobiles. There has not been a need to develop a Crime Watch.

The Hartleys were one of the first residents of Crosby Heights in the first development of the subdivision. Given that, they have historical knowledge and a rapport with others in the neighborhood. The Hartleys are a White heterosexual married couple in their mid-fifties and are employed full time. They have adult children who no longer live with them. Their daughter (Rebecca) and her family (wife and twin sons) live on the same street as the couple. The Hartleys have self-appointed themselves as community leaders and are seen as influencers and powerbrokers as it relates to the business of the HOA. Mr. Daniel Hartley serves on the board of directors as the vice president. Their daughter, Rebecca, was one of the board members who did not finish their term but remained involved by attending meetings and engaging with the social media group. Mrs. Linda Hartley is not a board member but is privy to information via her husband and daughter. She is quite vocal in the social media group and likes to spearhead social gatherings for the neighbors to get to know each other. Although the family is active in the HOA and community social media group, the intent and effect of their involvement within the neighborhood have created a divide among residents.

As residents become acquainted with the neighborhood and the community at large, they join the Crosby Heights social media group. This group is an unofficial means to build community, seek referrals and recommendations for services, and become familiar with those in the neighborhood. It is common for members to ask questions and share information regarding things such as lost pets, community events, neighborhood gatherings, or misplaced food or package delivery. The social media group is also an avenue for residents to field questions to the HOA officers or receive guidance on certain topics. The social media group is monitored by the Hartley family. When the HOA is under scrutiny, or residents provide feedback that the Hartley family doesn't agree with, dialogue leads to heightened tensions and becomes emotionally charged. Although most of the group agrees with the Hartleys, there's a small group of residents taunted and shamed for sharing perspectives and experiences different from the Hartleys. The inability to appreciate the different values and beliefs of neighbors shows implicit biases that exist within the neighborhood.

Dominique Smith is an African American, middle-aged female who is new to the city and the neighborhood. She purchased her home in the last development and is on the last street of the neighborhood. Before moving to River Moss, Dominique lived in other states with neighborhoods that had an active HOA. She has experience participating in the neighborhood association and remains active in the HOA, where she is the landlord of a house. Initially, Dominique was excited to move to a new neighborhood with an emerging HOA. She thought this would be an excellent opportunity to meet people and pay it forward by sharing her experiences from previous neighborhoods. After attending a couple of meetings, Dominique's experience and advice were not welcomed by the HOA officers and neighbors. Dominique was not acknowledged by the HOA president in meetings, and when she was allowed to speak, her comments were acknowledged by silence and a quick dismissal. The more Dominique contributed to the social media group or HOA meetings, the more she felt like an outsider. In addition to being one of the few African Americans in the neighborhood, she questioned if her race and gender contributed to the distanced reception from her neighbors.

Dominique did not let the unwelcoming environment deter her from participating in conversations with neighbors she met on the street. There would be neighborly exchanges of people asking for recommendations or sharing information in private exchanges after an HOA meeting or via direct message on social media. A core group would also share information during the summer months about Food Truck events and seasonal yard sales. There was a general sense of community despite the HOA not operating as the governing body of the Crosby Heights neighborhood.

Unfortunately, the formed sense of community would be interrupted by the Hartley family and their supporters. Concerned neighbors use the social media platform to report suspicious behaviors and to report problems that require the attention of the HOA. In particular, the reports are often of "suspicious" persons of color walking or driving through the neighborhood. Dominique has tried to provide a different perspective, such as slow drivers may be delivery or ride-share drivers looking for an address. However, any explanation is met with resistance and fearmongering that neighbors should be alert, aware, and protect themselves at all costs with armed weapons. This troubles Dominique more than ever. She is single and sometimes walks around the neighborhood for exercise. What if a resident doesn't recognize her and threatens her? What if an innocent driver is looking for a yard sale or a food truck and is harmed?

What if the police are involved and she (or a Black neighbor) is arrested? What if a neighbor takes matters into their own hands? Dominique has tried to use her voice to educate about implicit biases and assumptions about people of color. She has spoken up about the number of Black and Brown people who have been killed by police. The Hartleys are vocal on social media to quell Dominique's reactions to perceived concerns and alarming tactics that they raise. The Hartley family spew accusations, resort to name-calling, and maintain that Dominique is overreacting because race has nothing to do with the comments on social media. Other neighbors have accused Dominique of staging her experiences and have asked her to refrain from the use of her "woke language" and "woke commentary." They further assert that they don't see color because they have Black friends and are not racists. Because the Hartleys have formed allegiances within the neighborhood and serve on the HOA board, several other residents support the Hartley family. Dominique insists that concerns about safety or unusual actions by unknown individuals, typically people of color, are not raised when a White person exhibits suspicious behavior or concerning activity. For example, there have been talks about a White male speeding excessively through the neighborhood, yet no one has formally complained or posted on Facebook. Dominique has expressed that she would appreciate equal thought and reporting of concerning behavior in the neighborhood. No one considers Dominique's point of view of being a Black woman in America and her lived experiences. The colorblindness of her neighbors poses potential harm and overall safety concerns. There is no intervention from the HOA as the governing entity of the neighborhood. The HOA can ensure neighborhood safety with a few intervention strategies, such as establishing safety guidelines, hosting safety meetings, or establishing a neighborhood watch program in collaboration with law enforcement. This would result in communication education and community education to include clear processes for reporting safety concerns to the appropriate entities. At present, there are no efforts to ensure that all neighborhood members have equitable experiences despite race, power, and privilege impacting those experiences (Daftary, 2020). The Crosby Heights HOA's actions to allow colorblind officers to serve as the "voice of the neighborhood" create an opportunity for covert and overt forms of racism and discrimination to occur. The unspoken expectation is to be neighborly, get along with one another, agree with the majority, and abide by the HOA covenants, although the officers have not made the covenants enforceable.

Color blindness, the idea that one should not see race to foster equality, often blurs the realities of White privilege, which allows White individuals to navigate society with advantages that people of color do not share (Bonilla-Silva, 2010). The Hartleys and other neighbors consistently dispel the stories of Black neighbors having a different experience in the neighborhood because of their skin color. Specifically, they denounce the idea that Blacks are treated with more suspicion by their neighbors. The Hartleys claim that they will never do such a thing, given that they have Black friends.

Such blindness to the lived experiences of people of color allows White neighbors like the Hartleys to navigate their lives with privilege. This dynamic is evident in the behavior of the Hartleys, who have installed an above-ground pool in defiance of the Crosby Heights covenants, asserting their right to enjoy their property without regard for community rules. Their actions reflect a broader pattern where White residents, like them, let their pets roam unleashed, violating HOA regulations without facing the consequences. These behaviors undermine the authority of the HOA and create an environment where rules are selectively enforced, raising significant concerns about the long-term vitality of the neighborhood. Such inequities threaten property values and diminish the community's appeal for future homeowners and renters of color, ultimately jeopardizing the sustainability of an inviting and inclusive neighborhood.

Social Work Practice Intervention

A group of concerned residents have pooled together their resources to work with a consultant who can best advise them on legal options to save Crosby Heights before someone is harmed or injured due to the lack of rule enforcement. The residents asked Dominique to join them because of her prior experiences of living in a community with a neighborhood association, then moving to a new subdivision that formed a new HOA, and most recently living where there was an established HOA. Moreover, she was invited to advance the voice of minoritized persons in the neighborhood. The concerned residents asked for guidance from the City of River Moss's Neighborhood Development Office. The Neighborhood Development Office is tasked with empowering neighborhoods with community development, neighborhood enrichment programs, and community engagement opportunities. Yolanda Booker was assigned as the community engagement specialist for the Crosby Heights neighborhood. Yolanda is Latina and was raised in River Moss. After completing her bachelor's and master's degrees, she returned to River Moss to give back to her community. Yolanda is a master's level social worker who has been deeply inspired by CRT in her work, using its principles to guide her interventions and strategies aimed at improving diversity, equity, inclusion, and justice in communities. She incorporates various strategies, such as conducting community needs assessments to gather input from underrepresented groups, ensuring that their voices shape the programs and services offered. Additionally, Yolanda implements community engagement initiatives that foster a sense of belonging among all residents, encouraging participation from diverse demographics. She also establishes opportunities for feedback and conducts periodic evaluations to measure the effectiveness and inclusivity of her interventions. By prioritizing these practices, Yolanda not only addresses systemic inequities but also creates an environment where all community members feel valued. She enjoys meeting residents and learning from their diverse viewpoints, recognizing that their experiences and insights are crucial to building a more inclusive community. Through her work, Yolanda aims to exemplify CRT in her practice by dismantling oppressive systems and groups and promoting social justice.

Yolanda began a fact-finding session and followed the steps of the helping process when working with mezzo and macro groups. She promptly identified the CRT tenet of the critique of liberalism to apply to the Crosby Heights HOA and residents. She met with the concerned citizen group to ascertain the key issues of concern. Additionally, she reached out to the HOA officers, the developer Larry Lee, and the HOA's attorney. Through a series of individual and group meetings, she was able to engage with the neighborhood to begin an ongoing assessment of areas to focus on. After gaining a full understanding of the various concerns and issues, her priority was to empower the HOA officers and residents to build an inclusive community by creating a functioning governing body that reflects different experiences. Yolanda immediately connected with Dominique. She could relate to her experiences. One of Yolanda's first recommendations was to discuss the concept of *White privilege* with the residents. She decided to start there in hopes that the HOA board and other White residents would understand the impact of their words and beliefs. White privilege can protect persons from the fear of hostility and violence that Dominique feels when she shares her perspective (McIntosh, 2019). Moreover, Yolanda wanted the residents to understand that White privilege is a complex term with a larger meaning and refers to systematic oppression because of one's race (McIntosh, 2019). As a part of Yolanda's empowering tactic, her approach was for the Crosby Heights residents to understand that rules and laws create different experiences based on a person's race and other dominant cultural forms.

Yolanda developed a six-week course titled "Unpacking Privilege and Building Community." Initially, the majority of residents did not want to accept that there were race-related issues because they feared that they would be considered racists in a town that has a history of race-related conflict. However, as a result of the course, Crosby Heights residents received implicit bias training. The HOA officers learned effective language to communicate with their attorney and how to obtain full ownership of the association so that they could begin enforcing the covenants by issuing fines and/or liens against homeowners. Yolanda's course was initially met with resistance from the Hartleys and their peers. The Hartleys tried their best to dissuade residents from attending. This wasn't unique for Yolanda. She provided incentives such as childcare, gift cards, and meals to influence members to take part. She increased communication and transparency with those whom she had built an alliance. Those residents encouraged their neighbors via Facebook and in person to attend the session. Once the Hartleys realized that they were outnumbered, the family started attending meetings.

The officers obtained skills to develop and execute a budget, provide minutes to residents, and create a neighborhood database to track homeowners versus renters. Additionally, Yolanda worked strategically with the board and residents to create a more inclusive and equitable governance framework. Together, they established anti-oppressive outcomes that promoted diverse representation on the board and in community discussions, fostering alliances and raising awareness about how everyday practices in the community can marginalize some homeowners.

The residents were able to form committees to plan neighborhood gatherings and to maintain green spaces. Those who were interested in becoming officers learned the basics of Robert's Rule of Order to facilitate timely meetings with a clear purpose by creating and providing access to a meeting agenda and supplemental documents, properly following the agenda while allowing time for reports, discussion, voting, and follow-up. This created a group of prepared and readily available officers who could view the covenants and ensure that they were ethically upheld.

Implications for Practice

The racial divide in the Crosby Heights subdivision demonstrates what can happen when those with privilege do not understand the realities of minority groups. Colorblindness connects with the critique of liberalism by emphasizing individualism and the notion that ignoring race will lead to equality, which overlooks the systemic inequalities and historical injustices that shape social dynamics

(Bonilla-Silva, 2010). This approach promotes a false understanding of justice, resisting the structural changes needed to address the true root causes of racial disparities, ultimately maintaining the status quo rather than fostering true equity. A fundamental flaw in liberalism is that concepts like colorblindness and incremental change allow the dominant culture to shape the outcome. As researchers, educators, and practitioners unpack the critique of liberalism tenet of CRT, there are three areas that Ashley and Paez (2015) highlight as skills from their study to practice as scholars of the CRT framework. The first is to build confidence and use culturally competent vocabulary to explore, understand, and communicate race, power, and privilege. An example of this is by acknowledging and understanding what the critique of liberalism is. Secondly, it is important to gain the ability to process the tension and discomfort that come with race-related issues, such as recognizing colorblindness or White privilege. There are topics within race, power, and privilege that can be uncomfortable. CRT teaches how to have critical conversations without feelings of guilt or embarrassment. Lastly, consider the cornerstone of social justice and its reach into practice. The overarching goal of anti-oppressive work is to strive for a completely just society, not an incrementally just society that is controlled by dominant groups. CRT allows practitioners and educators to acknowledge social justice issues that are seen within conversations of race, power, and privilege. Using CRT as a framework provides individuals with the skills to recognize social justice issues and create effective solutions for the complex challenges associated with them. These challenges include resistance to and misinterpretation of CRT and its tenets and institutional barriers that hinder diversity, equity, and inclusive practices.

Acknowledging and understanding White privilege can make persons accountable (McIntosh, 2019). White privilege is something that is not as easily noticeable to someone who can easily navigate life with a particular set of advantages and opportunities. Ladson-Billings and Tate (1995) provide an excellent discussion of the intersection of race and property as a social construct for understanding inequity. There are rights of disposition, rights to use and enjoyment, reputation, status property, and the absolute right to exclude. Through the critique of liberalism, which challenges colorblindness, there is a notion that there are laws to allow minority races to purchase homes, own land, and have other equitable resources. However, there are overt and covert laws that are regulated or monitored by privileged White groups to allow accessible means for social and economic gain for the dominant group. Considering that there are other points of intersectionality, such as class, religion, ethnic status, or geographic location, this further complicates a person of color's ability to have laws in favor of them (McIntosh, 2019). Practitioners, scholars, and educators should be mindful that race is at the root of how laws are structured and implemented. The Great Divide in the Crosby Heights neighborhood and the application of the critique of liberalism demonstrate that by failing to address systemic inequalities and prioritizing White privilege and individualism over collective responsibility, the community perpetuates divisions that undermine true equity and social justice.

Discussion Questions

1. What examples of colorblindness are reflected in the case?
2. How does the critique of liberalism (specifically challenging colorblindness) offer an alternative perspective to help the Crosby Heights HOA?
3. The new housing development offers expanded opportunities for a diverse range of residents to relocate to River Moss, along with an increase in available homes for prospective homeowners. How does the neighborhood's colorblindness overlook or undermine equity and equality in the neighborhood?
4. What are the implications of the critique of liberalism for the future of democracy and social justice movements?
5. How can critiquing liberalism (specifically challenging colorblindness) help with new social justice movements?

REFERENCES

Abrams, L. S., & Moio, J. A. (2009). Critical race theory and the cultural competence dilemma in social work education. *Journal of Social Work Education, 45*(2), 245–261. https://doi.org/10.5175/JSWE.2009.200700109

Ashley, W., & Paez, J. (2015). Enhancing strengths-based social work pedagogy: From cultural competence to critical race theory. *The International Journal of Interdisciplinary Educational Studies, 10*(4), 15–25. https://doi.org/10.18848/2327-011x/cgp/v10i04/53291

Bonilla-Silva, E. (2010). *Racism without racists: Color-blind racism and the persistence of racial inequality in the United States* (3rd ed.). Rowman & Littlefield.

Daftary, A. (2020). Critical race theory: An effective framework for social work research. *Journal of Ethnic & Cultural Diversity in Social Work, 29*(6), 439–454. https://doi.org/10.1080/15313204.2018.1534223

Kolivoski, K. M., Weaver, A., & Constance-Huggins, M. (2014). Critical race theory: Opportunities for applications in social work practice and policy. *Families in Society, 95*(4), 269–276. https://doi.org/10.1606/1044-3894.2014.95.36

Ladson Billings, G., & Tate, W. (1995). Toward a critical race theory of education. *Teachers College Record (1970), 97*(1), 47–68. https://doi.org/10.1177/016146819509700104

McIntosh, P. (2019). White privilege: Unpacking the invisible knapsack (1989) 1. In *On privilege, fraudulence, and teaching as learning* (pp. 29–34). Routledge. https://doi.org/10.4324/9781351133791-4

Ortiz, L., & Jani, J. (2010). Critical race theory: A transformational model for teaching diversity. *Journal of Social Work Education, 46*(2), 175–193. https://doi.org/10.5175/JSWE.2010.200900070

CASE 4.5

You Can't Budget Your Way Out of Racism

How the Endemic Nature of Racism Perpetuates Financial Instability among Black Single Mothers

EMILY C. PATE

Racism being endemic is a tenet of critical race theory that describes how everyday, ordinary, and woven racism is in society. According to Sulé (2020), "racism is embedded into the fabric of our institutions, policies, and practices. Therefore, it creates a social structure that reifies and reproduces advantages for those categorized as white and disadvantages for minoritized groups" (pp. 2-3). This case study will explore how the endemic nature of racism affects Black women, specifically, Black single mothers.

Case Study

Rachel is a twenty-four-year-old, white social worker who recently graduated and obtained her first job at a local nonprofit called Change for Good. She wasn't sure what area of social work she wanted to go into, but knew she wanted to work at the macro level to address community-wide and systemic issues. She landed herself at Change for Good, which focused on addressing financial instability. Rachel had never thought about how big of an issue this was in the community; she had grown up with two working, middle-class parents and they all had lived a very comfortable life. She always woke up to piles of Christmas presents on Christmas morning, her parents took her on week-long vacations every summer, and she even took cello classes outside of school. The idea of learning about financial instability at the community level intrigued her.

Within a few weeks of starting and learning office and program procedures, she felt ready to begin working with clients. Her supervisor, Martha, suggested sitting in on a few weeks of meetings before jumping into leading sessions, and Rachel agreed. She then sat in on her first session with her supervisor and a client named Monet.

Monet is a forty-three-year-old, Black, single working mother of three. She came from a working family with two parents and five siblings and remembers having to go without essentials often. Some weeks, her parents couldn't afford the utility bills and other weeks, they mostly had bread and butter to eat for dinner because they couldn't afford groceries after paying all the other expenses. She never got the chance to see the ocean, as vacations were never in the budget for her family. Her parents worked very hard, but she remembers hearing them cry when they were unable to provide their children with more than a bag of fruit for Christmas.

During the session Rachel was observing, Monet was noticeably distressed and frustrated. When asked about this, she simply exclaimed, "What's the point of even trying to get ahead! Me and my children will never have a house! We can barely afford rent! It takes everything I have just to keep them fed; rent and food takes my whole paycheck!" Martha tried to sympathize with Monet and acknowledge how difficult it can be to "get ahead," when it takes everything just to survive. She asked Monet if she still wished to work on her budget during this session, to which Monet got up and exited the room saying, "What's the point? There's nothing left to budget – you can't budget your way out of poverty!"

Rachel was stunned. She had never considered this before. She felt concerned for Monet as well as for her children. "Couldn't she apply for the Supplemental Nutrition Assistance Program (SNAP) to help her with food costs?" Rachel inquired. Martha let out a sigh, "She makes too much money." Rachel didn't understand how this was possible and became extremely frustrated herself; "What do you mean she makes too much? She is obviously struggling!" Martha explained how most programs determine eligibility of services based on the federal poverty line, which doesn't reflect a living wage and hasn't been updated based on inflation in several years. Rachel was even more discouraged to hear that, even if someone is over the limit by a single dollar, they are automatically ineligible for services. "This is the case for many of the families we work with," Martha explained, "They are caught in the gap of making 'too much' for public assistance but in reality, they are struggling to make ends meet."

For Rachel, this was an undeniable trend of working hard but being unable to make ends meet that she observed over the next several weeks. She also realized that a vast majority of clients with this issue were Black single mothers who faced multiple barriers to sustainable employment and financial stability. She started to wonder why it was so much more difficult for Black individuals, specifically Black single mothers, to be financially stable. Rachel remembered learning about CRT in her social work classes and asked Martha if they could set aside time to discuss this trend and how CRT could be applied to enrich the work already being done with the clients at Change for Good.

Context: Why Are Black Mothers Struggling?

Currently, the feminization of poverty affects millions of women worldwide. Black women, who are oppressed based on their race as well as their gender, face additional barriers to escaping poverty. Due to gender and racial bias and inequality, Black women are more susceptible to poverty than men and white women, and experience a lack of control, choice, opportunities, and resources necessary to provide for themselves and their families.

According to Melo (2019), the feminization of poverty refers to the process in which multidimensional cultural, social, and structural factors cause and exacerbate poverty among women and girls. Gender and cultural norms, gender bias, and gender-based discrimination in the workplace are examples in society that contribute to the perpetuation of poverty for women. These factors are often subtle or intrinsic, so they become endemic and difficult to address. Additionally, Black single mothers face added barriers and discrimination based on their race, which compound with discrimination based on their gender (Few & Allen, 2020). This layering of discrimination and oppression creates a unique set of challenges for Black mothers trying to provide for their families.

Applying Critical Race Theory

Oftentimes, the ways in which Black women experience racism and discrimination goes unnoticed. Instead, they are blamed for their financial and living situations without any context given to the hidden and endemic barriers they face to financial stability. CRT addresses this in the tenet racism is endemic. The concept of race and racism being endemic means that they are deeply woven into the fabric of society, so they can easily be missed if not intentionally addressed. The implications of this are that racism becomes woven into society through policies, workplaces, and ways of life, so intrinsically that it is accepted as the norm.

Given racism is endemic, it has very alarming consequences. For example, in 2021, full-time, year-round working women earned 84 percent of what their male counterparts earned, on average, according to the Census Bureau's most recent analysis. This gap is widened when race is considered. Looking across racial and ethnic groups, there is a large disparity separating the earnings of Black women from the earnings of white men and white women. In 2022, Black women earned 70 cents per every dollar that white men earn, on average, compared to 84 cents per dollar for all women (Aragão, 2023). This is true even when educational attainment and experience is accounted for, meaning the difference in pay is based on something more discreet and even implicit.

An implicit barrier to financial stability and career advancement is known as "The Broken Rung." This concept states that Black individuals face lower rates of career advancement than other racial groups, making them less likely to be promoted to management/higher-paying positions (Guy, 2020). This is caused by internal employment discrimination, where white managers are more likely to hire, promote, and grant a pay raise to someone who is the same race as them – perpetuating the cycle of racial prejudice and discrimination in the workplace.

Additionally, Black American employment is concentrated in low-paying jobs such as cashiers and janitors – job positions where the worker is more likely to be financially unstable. This is largely attributed to hiring discrimination where Black Americans are less likely to be hired in higher-paying jobs, again due to racial discrimination. In the 2003 Bertrand and Mullainathan study, hiring discrimination was found in the form of name bias. Names like "Emily" are more likely to get callbacks after submitting an online or mail-in application as opposed to those with names associated with Black women such as "Lakisha." This study demonstrates the endemic nature of hiring discrimination, where the implicit biases of the hiring team prevent Black women from ever receiving a chance at sustainable, higher-paying employment.

A Macro Intervention for a Macro-Scale Issue

After an in-depth discussion with her supervisor, Rachel felt driven to try and address the endemic nature of racism in her organization's work. She knew that she came from a place of privilege and had the opportunity to use research and policy changes to address racism and the barriers to financial stability for Black mothers. She proposed that her organization make this issue a point of advocacy in their work, and that they use their position in the circle of nonprofits to make systemic, macro-level change. Otherwise, Black Americans, and in particular, Black single mothers, would never have the same chance as others at getting ahead financially. As Monet stated, you cannot budget your way out of poverty, not when racism infiltrates the very systems, employment opportunities, and work environments that directly affect one's ability to work and earn money. Therefore, Rachel and Martha acknowledged that it is imperative to address the specific barriers to financial stability and equality that CRT highlights, as these issues are race-driven and therefore require a race-driven solution. Accordingly, Rachel and Martha used research conducted by Thomas et al. (2023) from *McKinsey and Company*, a global management consulting firm, to adapt the following plan with the goal of putting race and gender at the center of addressing systemic barriers to financial stability.

When considering how to make a systemic difference in employers' approach to hiring, promotion, and employee retainment for women, the following recommendations were made by Thomas et al.: ensure that women obtain the tools they need to become managers, such as leadership training, sponsorship, and high-profile assignments; set and publicize a bold goal to increase the number of women at the management level; set diversity targets for hiring and promotions to ensure that the processes work to shape employee representation; require diverse slates of candidates for hiring and promotions at the management level; establish clear and consistent evaluation criteria before review processes begin; require unconscious bias training for employees who are involved in entry-level hiring and performance reviews (Thomas et al., 2023).

Martha and Rachel adapted this approach to center race as a factor, as opposed to primarily focusing on gender, to more adequately address the disparities Black women face in achieving financial stability. They use their own organization's experience as well as national and local statistics to highlight the need to incorporate these recommendations into employment practices for local businesses. They continue to provide statistics on the gender and race pay gaps and advocate for fair pay. They have received mixed reactions, but they continue this work because they know life cannot improve for their clients until this issue is addressed on a macro level. Through a grant fund they have established, they now provide free implicit bias training as well as Diversity, Equity, and Inclusion (DEI) training as an incentive to companies who wish to pursue these recommendations but are hesitant to spend company dollars on such. They see more and more businesses and companies becoming interested in learning the intentions and implications of CRT and embrace the opportunity of providing this education. They are confident that, if those in positions of power and privilege join them in implementing these macro-level interventions, there can be positive change in even the most endemic forms of racism.

Implications for Practice: How CRT Enriches Social Work Interventions

Given the endemic nature of racism and the systemic ways it can affect clients, social workers should make intentional efforts to be aware of the many ways race-based oppression can affect clients. It is, therefore, essential that social workers educate themselves on systemic and interpersonal ways in which racism affects their practice with Black clients. Social workers, specifically those who work on the macro level, have a responsibility to work towards dismantling institutions and practices that contribute to the oppression of Black individuals. This includes participating in trainings on diversity and anti-oppressive practices, assessing organizations for discriminatory practices and policies, and collaborating with organizations to implement social policy changes (Sulé, 2020).

It is also crucial for social workers to be aware of their own lived experiences, potential implicit biases, and the power imbalance that can exist in their work with Black individuals. Social workers should be conscientious to not impose their beliefs onto clients and to let the client lead discussions and recognize they are the expert of their own lived experience (Sulé, 2020).

Though the recommendations provided by McKinsey and Company were a good place to start, Rachel and Martha know from CRT the importance of continuing to find ways to tweak these to place race at the center of these interventions. Addressing gender-based discrimination is crucial for Black women to have a more equitable chance of being financially stable, but it is also imperative to ensure race is at the center, as it has such a large impact on the everyday operations of places of employment and everyday life for Black individuals. Now, Rachel and Martha consider race in every interaction with clients to properly address their concerns and validate their difficulties. Monet and other clients now have the validation of knowing it is not their fault they cannot budget their way out of poverty, because they cannot budget themselves out of racism. Clients also know that Rachel and Martha will continue advocating to address racism even where it is endemic and often left unaddressed. They continue to work on the macro level to create and promote policy and system-level changes to the hiring process as well as the race and gender pay gaps in their community. Rachel and Martha now attend public policy day conventions as well as networking opportunities to build relationships with their local government officials and even state senators. They often provide research-driven cases to these officials and advocate for policies to be implemented that require businesses to address racial inequality in the workplace. They wish to continue this work and bring more individuals in on the work so that, one day, these recommendations and interventions can become not only common practice but required practices by law.

Discussion Questions

1. If Rachel and Martha were to only focus on gender-based discrimination and inequity, how would that affect Black individuals, like Monet, they are trying to help?

2. What are some other interventions that organizations or businesses can adopt that could further address racism in the workplace?
3. Reflect on how white privilege can affect a social worker's perspective on financial issues and racial inequality.
4. What are some other endemic ways that Black individuals face racial discrimination in everyday life?

REFERENCES

Aragão, C. (2023). Gender Pay Gap in U.S. Hasn't Changed Much in Two Decades. PEW Research Center. www.pewresearch.org/short-reads/2023/03/01/gender-pay-gap-facts/

Bertrand, M., & Mullainathan, S. (2003). Are Emily and Greg More Employable Than Lakisha and Jamal? A Field Experiment on Labor Market Discrimination. National Bureau of Economic Research. https://doi.org/10.3386/w9873

Few, D. A. L., & Allen, K. R. (2020). Gender, feminist, and intersectional perspectives on families: A decade in review. *Journal of Marriage & Family, 82*(1), 326–345. https://doi.org/10.1111/jomf.12638

Guy, S. (2020). Fixing the "broken rung" in the ladder to success. *Magazine of the Society of Women Engineers, 66*(2), 42–45. www.swe.org/wp-content/uploads/2021/08/FINAL_SWESOW2020-links-1.pdf#page = 44

Kochhar, R. (2023). The Enduring Grip of the Gender Pay Gap. PEW Research Center. www.pewresearch.org/social-trends/2023/03/01/the-enduring-grip-of-the-gender-pay-gap/

Melo, C. L. (2019). The feminization of poverty: A brief analysis of gender issues and poverty among women and girls. *The Canadian Journal of Critical Nursing Discourse, 1*(1), 73–81. https://doi.org/10.25071/2291-5796.6

Sulé, V. T. (2020). Critical race theory. *Encyclopedia of Social Work.* https://doi.org/10.1093/acrefore/9780199975839.013.1329

Thomas, R., Fairchild, C., Cardazone, G., Cooper, M., Fielding-Singh, P., Noble-Tolla, M., Burton, A., Krivkovich, A., Yee, L., Field, E., Robinson, N., & Kuegele, S. (2023) Women in the Workplace. McKinsey and Company. www.mckinsey.com/~/media/mckinsey/featured%20insights/diversity%20and%20inclusion/women%20in%20the%20workplace%202024%20the%2010th%20anniversary%20report/women-in-the-workplace-2024.pdf?utm_source = chatgpt.com

Index

Adelanta Mental Health Agency, 70
Advancing Marginalized Voices, 6, 54, 150
āinabased (land-based) community building, 146
Aloha ʻāina, 136, 138, 147
"Angry Black Woman" Stereotype, 54
Antiracism, 158
Antiretroviral Therapy, 22
Anxiety, 53

Bipolar I Disorder, 21
Black Girls Equity Alliance, 91
Blind community, 128
Broken Rung, 183
Brown vs. Board of Education, 4, 125

Centering the voice of the other, 136
Child welfare services, 97, 105
Children and Youth Justice Center, 82
Children, Youth, and Families Services (CYFS), 33-34
Chosen family, 119, 121
Chronic Stress, 24
Cognitive Writing Strategies, 55
Collective Trauma, 47
Color-blindness, 164, 172, 174, 176
Community practices
 kalo cultivation (taro), 136, 138-139, 141-142
Council on Social Work Education (CSWE), 6
Counter Storytelling, 88, 139
Critical Race Theory, 3
Critical self-reflexivity, 131
Critique of liberalism, 72
CRT challenges, 7
CRT concepts
 Advancing marginalized voices, 6, 54, 150
 Antiracism, 158

Centering the voice of the other, 136
Counter storytelling, 88, 139
Critical self-reflexivity, 131
Critique of liberalism, 72
 Color-blindness, 164, 172, 174, 176
 Eurocentric culture, 25
 Interest convergence, 4, 125, 133
 Intersectionality, 5, 42, 47, 86, 103, 108
 Liberalism and the neutrality of law, 4
 Racism as endemic, 3, 18, 25, 179, 182, 185
 Social constructivism, 4, 112-113
 White privilege, 5, 172, 176

Dating violence, vi, 11, 150-151
Decolonization, 139
Department of Juvenile Justice Services, 82
Deserving poor, 66
Distress tolerance, 54
Drapetomania, 28

Educational policy and Accreditation standard, 6, 160
Emotional liberation circle, 55
Epidemiology
 Home births, 30
 Homelessness, 48
 Juvenile justice system, 84
 Maternal mortality, 29, 35
 Neonatal jaundice, 32
 St. Bernadette County, 81
 Welfare participants, 62
 Youth incarceration, 85
Eurocentric culture, 25
Evidence-based interventions, 71

Family preservation services, 98
Feminization of poverty, 182
Foreign aid, 131, 133

Foster care, 98
Framework, theory, pedagogy
  Indigenous communities
    āinabased (land-based) community building, 147
    Aloha ʻāina, 138
    Decolonization, 139
    Kanaka ʻŌiwi CRT/KanakaCrit, 138, 140
    kūpuna (wisdom of elders), 136, 139
    Mālama ʻāina, 138
    Native Hawaiian epistemology, 137

Garifuna, 126
Gender transition, 40
Gender/sexuality
  Black queer community, 119
  Black transgender, 115
  LGBTQ+ adults, 119
  LGBTQQIA2S+ youth, 151
  Transgender, 48, 119
Gender-affirming surgery, 40
Geographic location
  Hawaii, 136
  New Mexico, vi, 11, 150
  St. Vincent and the Grenadines, 126
Gwen's Girls, 91

Hawaiian renaissance, 140
Health condition or disease
  Antiretroviral therapy, 22
  Anxiety, 53
  Bipolar I Disorder, 21
  Chronic stress, 24
  Gender transition, 40
  Gender-affirming surgery, 40
  HIV, 24
  Post Traumatic Stress Disorder, 21, 24
  Protective factors, 22
  Stroke, 115
Healthcare
  Medical abuse, 30
  Medical neglect investigation, 31
Hip-hop Psychology, 55
Historical event
  Law & policy
    Brown vs. Board of Education, 4, 125

Renaissance
  Hawaiian renaissance, 140
Social movement
  Aloha ʻāina, 136, 147
HIV, 24
Homeless shelters, 48

Immigrant experience, 50
Interest convergence, 4, 125, 133
Intersectionality, 5, 42, 47, 86, 103, 108

Juvenile courts, 90
Juvenile justice system, 84

Kalinago, 126
Kanaka ʻŌiwi CRT/KanakaCrit, 138, 140
kūpuna (wisdom of elders), 136, 139

La Soufrière, 126
LGBTQ+ adults, 119
LGBTQQIA2S+ Youth, 151
Liberalism and the neutrality of law, 4
Liberation psychology, 55

Mālama ʻāina, 138
Medical abuse, 30
Medical mistrust, 29
Medical neglect investigation, 31

Native Hawaiian epistemology, 137
Neonatal jaundice, 31, 33

Organizations
  Community organization
    Adelanta Mental Health Agency, 70
    Gwen's Girls, 91
    Umoja Pregnancy Center, 32
  For-profit
    Work opportunity center, 61
  Non-profit
    Hoʻokuaʻāina, 136
  Social services and public health agencies
    Child welfare services, 97, 105
    Children and Youth Justice Center, 82
    Children, Youth, and Families Services (CYFS), 33–34

Organizations (cont.)
   Department of Juvenile Justice Services, 82
   Foster care, 98
   State's Department of Human Services, 62
   Supplemental Nutrition Assistance Program, 181
   Temporary Assistance for Needy Families, 67
Outpatient therapy, 56

People
   Scholars
      Bell, Derrick, 3
      Collins, Patricia Hill, 5
      Crenshaw, Kimberlé, 5
      Delgado, Richard, 3
      McIntosh, Peggy, 5, 67
Post Traumatic Stress Disorder, 21, 24
Problem externalization, 56
Protective factors, 22
Psychosocial interventions
   Cognitive writing strategies, 55
   Distress tolerance, 54
   Emotional Liberation Circle, 55
   Hip-hop psychology, 55
   Liberation psychology, 55
   Outpatient therapy, 56
   Problem externalization, 56

Racial scrutiny, 36
Racial/ethnic group
   Black single mothers, 179-180
   Black, Indigenous, and other People of Color, 47
   Black, Indigenous, Latine and Youth of Color (BILYC), 151
   Indigenous Caribs, 126
   Indigenous communities
      Caribs, 126
   Native Hawaiian, 135
Racism, 18
Racism as endemic, 3, 18, 25, 179, 182, 185

Sandwich generation, 63
Social constructivism, 4, 112-113
Social issue
   Blind community, 128
   Broken Rung, 183
   Dating violence, vi, 11, 150-151
   Disaster relief/recovery, 127, 133
   Families
      Black mothers, 179-180
      Child abuse/neglect, 98
   Feminization of poverty, 182
   Global health and humanitarian ethics
      Foreign aid, 131, 133
      White Savior, 131
   Health disparities
      Homeless shelters, 49
      Racial scrutiny, 36
   Inequity drivers
      Deserving poor, 66
      Sanctioning Black, 65
      Social welfare vs. social control, 84
      Undeserving poor, 66
      Welfare sanctioning, 62, 65
      White privilege, 65, 67
      Workplace racial disparities, 53
   Justice system
      Girls in the Juvenile Justice System, 84
      Girls of color, 88, 91
      Juvenile Courts, 83, 90
   Medical racism
      Collective trauma, 47
      Drapetomania, 28
      Medical mistrust, 29
      Neonatal jaundice, 31, 33
      Portraying Black people as disease prone, 30
      Tuskegee Syphilis Study, 29
   Natural disaster/environmental justice
      La Soufrière, 126
      The HOA (Homeowner's Association), 165
Social welfare vs. social control, 84
Social work approach
   Council on Social Work Education (CSWE), 6
   Culturally responsive approach, 49
   Educational Policy and Accreditation Standards (EPAS), 7

Resources
    Domestic violence shelter, 44
    Emergency shelter, 44
    Temporary solution, 49
State's Department of Human Services, 62
Storytelling tradition, 88
Stroke, 115
Supplemental Nutrition Assistance Program, 181
Support programs
    Natural disaster/environmental justice
        Disaster relief/recovery, 127
Support programs
    Black Girls Equity Alliance, 91
    Family preservation services, 98
    Temporary Assistance for Needy Families, 62
    'We Got Y'all', 71

Temporary Assistance for Needy Families, 62, 67
The HOA (Homeowner's Association), 165

Transgender, 48, 119
Tuskegee Syphilis Study, 29

Umoja Pregnancy Center, 32
Undeserving poor, 66

'We Got Y'all', 71
Welfare sanctioning, 62, 65
White privilege, 3, 5, 65, 67, 172, 176
White Savior, 131
White supremacy culture characteristics, 73
    Color evasiveness, 76
    'Fear of Open Conflict', 74
    Individualism, 75
    Objectivity, worship of the written word, 74
    Paternalism, power hoarding, one right way, 75
    Quantity over quality, 75
    Sense of urgency, 74
Work Opportunity Center, 61
Workplace racial disparities, 53

Youth incarceration, 85

For EU product safety concerns, contact us at Calle de José Abascal, 56–1°, 28003 Madrid, Spain or eugpsr@cambridge.org.

www.ingramcontent.com/pod-product-compliance
Ingram Content Group UK Ltd.
Pitfield, Milton Keynes, MK11 3LW, UK
UKHW022136240226
468380UK00018B/330